KILLERS
IN THE
FAMILY

Berkley titles by Robert L. Snow

SLAUGHTER ON NORTH LASALLE

KILLERS IN THE FAMILY

KILLERS
IN THE
FAMILY

Inside a Real Family of
Criminals Bound by Blood

ROBERT L. SNOW

BERKLEY BOOKS, NEW YORK

THE BERKLEY PUBLISHING GROUP
Published by the Penguin Group
Penguin Group (USA) LLC
375 Hudson Street, New York, New York 10014

USA • Canada • UK • Ireland • Australia • New Zealand • India • South Africa • China

penguin.com

A Penguin Random House Company

KILLERS IN THE FAMILY

A Berkley Book / published by arrangement with the author

For information, address: The Berkley Publishing Group,
a division of Penguin Group (USA) LLC,
375 Hudson Street, New York, New York 10014.

ISBN: 978-0-425-26608-3

PUBLISHING HISTORY
Berkley premium edition / July 2014

PRINTED IN THE UNITED STATES OF AMERICA

10 9 8 7 6 5 4 3 2 1

Cover design by Jane Hammer.
Cover art: *Girl Behind Bars* © Matej Hudovernik/Shutterstock;
Portrait of Large Family © RimDream/Shutterstock.
Interior text design by Laura K. Corless.

For Joy and Julian Bertram
and James and Luke Mullett
with love

FOREWORD

H is dream had finally come true.

At a little before 9:00 A.M. on June 18, 2012, retired detective sergeant Roy West sat outside of Criminal Court 2 in downtown Indianapolis. The dream he'd had for more than twenty-six years—of finally seeing justice for thirteen-year-old Dawn Marie Stuard—was at last coming true. West looked down at the thick folder he held in his lap. Dawn's case had never left his thoughts for the last twenty-six years, and he had never given up hope that this day might finally come. Even after retiring from the Indianapolis Police Department five years earlier, West had kept the file and looked through it frequently. Then, when he began working as an investigator for the Marion County Prosecutor's Office, he had continued to revisit the case over and over in the hope that something new would pop up. West would reread the interviews and notes from his investigation, thinking back over the years and wondering what he might have missed. He had talked with prosecutors a number of times over the years, asking what they felt the case needed in order to make it viable for prosecution. West had had a long career with many successes, but this particular case still haunted him.

West had served on the Indianapolis Police Department for more than thirty-five years. He'd joined in 1972 and had held various positions within the department until he transferred to the Homicide Branch in 1986, where he'd found his niche and served until his retirement in 2007. Although West was much too modest a man to ever believe it, he became something of a legend during his time as a homicide investigator, not only for solving many, many murder cases, but even more notably, for solving a number of cases that other homicide detectives had labeled unsolvable. He had even closed the North LaSalle Street murder case, unquestionably the most infamous murder case in Indianapolis history, which had lain unsolved for thirty years before West began looking into it.[1]

But even with all of his successes, the one case he couldn't solve but had never given up on had been the Dawn Marie Stuard murder case. It had been his first case as a homicide investigator. More important, though,

---

1 See author's previous book, *Slaughter on North LaSalle*, for a full accounting of that case.

to West, it had been a case that involved a totally innocent thirteen-year-old girl. West could never get that out
of his mind. A young child just starting out in life had
been brutally murdered, and even though West knew
without a doubt who had committed the murder, he had
never been able to gather the evidence necessary to bring
the case to trial.

For the tenth time, West looked down at his watch.
The jury selection would be starting soon. The former
detective couldn't help but be excited that modern science had finally done what he had been unable to do in
1986. Modern science had produced the evidence that
West had searched for for over a quarter of a century.
Still, along with the excitement, West could also feel his
stomach roll with uncertainty. He had taken part in dozens and dozens of jury trials during his career and knew
that the outcome of a jury trial was never certain. Would
the new evidence be enough? Would it convince the
jury to convict Dawn Marie Stuard's murderer?

After a moment, West pushed his worries aside, since
there was nothing he could do about them, and began
reviewing his notes on the case again. He didn't want to
look confused or uncertain when he testified. Thumbing
through the folder, West went back to 1986.

ONE

Thirteen-year-old Dawn Marie Stuard disappeared on March 16, 1986.

At the time, the Stuard family lived in the 1600 block of North Dequincy Street on the east side of Indianapolis, Indiana, but Dawn's father, Ted Stuard, had been working at a propane company in Ohio and was researching the possibility of purchasing Apollo Propane in Dayton. Before he and his wife, Sandy, could manage the purchase, though, they needed to be certain that they would have enough contracts in place to assure the business would prosper, so Ted and Sandy would drive to Ohio during the week, leaving their daughter, Dawn, in Indianapolis with an aunt, then come home every weekend. It was a bit stressful on the family, but Ted hoped it was just a short-term necessity.

"It was just a temporary thing," Ted said. "We didn't

want to have to take Dawn out of school until we were absolutely sure about moving permanently to Ohio."

More than anything, Ted's dream was to give his family a financially secure future. Once he and his wife owned the propane company, then this could all come true. They would make much more money and be able to provide a higher quality of life for their family. There would be no more traveling back and forth to Ohio every week. There would be no more evenings apart. There would be no more of these long drives and of living at a motel. Although Dawn would have to change schools, they knew she was a very sociable little girl who made friends easily. They felt certain she would make the transition smoothly. Ted and Sandy both looked eagerly toward the point when their family would be together all of the time. Yes, things were soon going to be great for the Stuard family.

On Sunday, March 16, 1986, Ted and Sandy rose early in the morning. Even though it was the weekend, they had to go back to Dayton to nail down the purchase of Apollo Propane. As usual, they had arranged for Sandy's sister, Ramona Collins, who lived just two blocks north of them, to watch Dawn that day. They left instructions with their daughter that, after she cleaned her room, she was to go straight to her Aunt Mona's house.

The day couldn't have looked brighter for Ted and Sandy as they left Indianapolis en route to Dayton. They were certain that Dawn *would* clean her room and then go straight to her aunt's house, just as they had told her to do. Dawn was an exceptionally good child who always minded her parents. She attended eighth grade at nearby

Forest Manor Elementary, had always gotten good grades, and got along well with her teachers and classmates. She had never really given her parents any problems at all. Ted and Sandy left for Ohio with no worries, only dreams of the great future awaiting them.

Later that morning, though, Dawn's Aunt Mona became concerned when her niece didn't show up as planned. Even if Dawn had poked around at home cleaning her room, she still should have made it to Mona's house by now. It wasn't so late yet that Mona panicked, but late enough that she started to worry—and as more time passed and Dawn still didn't arrive, Mona became even more concerned. She sent her nineteen-year-old son, Wesley Collins, down to his cousin's house to see if Dawn was there. She wasn't. At 3:00 P.M., Mona called Ted and Sandy in Ohio and told them she hadn't seen Dawn yet but that she had some more places to check and she would call them back. Mona then had Wesley ask around the neighborhood whether anyone had seen Dawn or knew where she was. Wesley stopped at every place he could think of that Dawn might be, but he couldn't find her. He heard from several people, however, that his cousin might be at the Reese house at 1428 North Bosart Street, just a few blocks away. Apparently, according to the people Wesley talked to, Dawn had been seen there several times before.

This information made Wesley very uncomfortable, his stomach a bit queasy. The Reese family had a bad reputation in the neighborhood. In addition to forty-three-year-old Paul Reese Sr. and forty-four-year-old Barbara

Reese, their four sons lived in the house: sixteen-year-old Paul Reese Jr., fifteen-year-old John Reese, fourteen-year-old Brian Reese, and thirteen-year-old Jeremy Reese. There were also two daughters: twelve-year-old Jenny and six-year-old Cynthia. People who lived nearby felt nothing was safe from being stolen by the four Reese boys. Because of the Reeses, no one in the neighborhood ever left anything of value sitting out in their yard.

Two of the Reese boys, Jeremy and John, had recently been arrested and were being held in the Indianapolis Juvenile Detention Center. Even the matriarch of the family, Barbara Reese, had once been convicted of embezzlement. But the Reese family also had a darker reputation than just for thievery. As most of the people living around there knew, the father, Paul Reese Sr., had been released a few years earlier from prison, where he had served time for trying to kill his then girlfriend. (That revelation had undoubtedly figured into the legal separation and divorce Barbara had filed for in 1979.) In 1986, Paul Reese Sr. lived mostly with his father but visited and stayed at the North Bosart house often.

Wesley couldn't believe that his little cousin Dawn would be at the Reese house. Why would she go somewhere like that? *Who knew what could happen to a child who went in there?* neighborhood parents would warn their children. A number of the parents in the neighborhood said that they gave their children strict orders to never go into the Reese house, and one woman with whom reporters later spoke said she'd told her daughter not to even walk close to the Reese house.

Even so, several people Wesley talked to said that Dawn had been there before, and that she might be there now. So of course, he had to check.

Wesley went to the Reese house and talked to two little girls playing out front. They said Dawn had been there but that she had left. Barbara Reese, the mother of the family, then appeared, and Wesley asked her if she had seen his cousin Dawn. He was told no, but something just didn't feel right about Barbara Reese's denial. It all seemed very nervous and edgy to him. Wesley managed to talk his way into the house, so that he could look around. He didn't find anything but would later say that the house gave him chills—as if it were a bad place, where bad things happened. Later that day, he returned several times and sat in a car near the Reese house, and even followed a visitor to the Reese house, a seventeen-year-old boy named Timothy Keller, to a nearby apartment and questioned him about Dawn. Timothy said he didn't know anything about where Dawn might be.

By the time Wesley returned after going to the Reese house, with no news of what had happened to Dawn, it was nearly 5:00 P.M., and Mona decided she needed to call her sister and brother-in-law again. She telephoned them in Dayton, and this time Ted and Sandy dropped everything and raced back home, a 115-mile trip.

"It was a two-and-a-half to three-hour drive to Indianapolis. But getting back home was the fastest trip I'd ever made from Dayton," Ted recalled. "I'm surprised I didn't get stopped by the police."

Ted and Sandy went first to Mona's house, then hurried home to see if they could find any clues there about what might have happened to their daughter. Ted could feel cold sweat running down his sides as he and Sandy stepped into their house, not knowing what to expect. Every nerve in his body seemed to be firing. They called over and over for Dawn but got no answer. They then began searching every room of their house. Nothing seemed alarming or out of place. Their house looked just as it had when they'd left that morning, except that Dawn's room was now tidy. Whatever had happened to her, she'd cleaned her room as instructed before leaving home.

Now icy, electric panic began setting in for Ted and Sandy. Where could Dawn be? Why hadn't she gone to Mona's house like she was supposed to? Ted and Sandy called every hospital and clinic where a sick or injured child might have been taken, but no one had a report of a child matching Dawn's description being brought in that day. They then got into their truck and began visiting Dawn's friends, asking if they had seen her or knew where she might be. No one did. The fear now began to squeeze them tighter and tighter with each failure to find any news about Dawn. They next began visiting all of the places they thought she might have gone.

"By the time we got back [home] it was getting close to dark," Ted recalled. "We went to all of her hangouts, all the places she might be. I was just trying to look for anything that might tell us where she was or had been. But it [was] getting later and later with no word about her."

Dawn's parents were worried sick about their little girl.

"She was a beautiful blond-haired, blue-eyed little girl," said Ted. "She didn't know an enemy or a stranger. She was friends with everybody. She liked to sing in the church choir. Dawn loved singing, even though she couldn't carry a note. At thirteen she had just recently discovered boys. She also liked to collect rocks. She was a good kid, a smart kid, did well in school. She had pen pals all over the world. She thought everyone was her friend. She never knew a stranger. Even as a baby she would walk up to people she didn't know and start talking. I could never get her not to do that. Everyone was a friend."

While their nephew Wesley had, of course, told them that several people had mentioned to him that Dawn might have been at the Reese house, it was one of the few places Ted and Sandy hadn't looked yet. But after their search turned up nothing, they decided that they had to try checking the Reese house on North Bosart.

"Wesley had already been to the Reese house three or four times trying to find Dawn because that was where a lot of people seemed to think she had gone," Ted said. "He did a lot of going back there and sitting in front of the Reese house. But there wasn't much he could do. Still, he had a feeling that Dawn was there."

Unlike most people in the neighborhood, Ted and Sandy didn't know about the Reese family's reputation. Since the Stuards spent so much time in Dayton, neither of them had picked up the neighborhood gossip. Even so, Ted had a hard time believing, no matter what people had told Wesley, that Dawn would go to the Reese house when they had told her specifically to go straight to her aunt Mona's. Dawn was a good little girl who had always done as she was told. However, Ted did recall that Dawn had once brought over to their house a little girl she was friends with at school, a girl named Jenny Reese. Jenny had seemed to Ted like a nice little girl.

Ted later found out that, unknown to him or Sandy, Dawn *had* been to the Reese house several times previously.

"I don't know why she kept it a secret from me, but probably because she was afraid I wouldn't approve of it once I found out about them," Ted said.

He also recalled that Dawn had been talking for some time about wanting to get a paper route so that she could earn some money. "She used to send little gifts to her pen pals, and I guess she wanted some extra money so she could do more of it," Ted recalled. He remembered Dawn mentioning to him that there was an older woman in the neighborhood who had a paper route she wanted to help on. Could that have been Mrs. Reese? Ted didn't know, and at the moment didn't care. He just wanted to find his daughter. Leaving Sandy and Mona behind to continue the search elsewhere, Ted, Wesley, and Wesley's girlfriend, Michelle Lynch, headed over to the Reeses.

When Ted and the others pulled up to the house on North Bosart Street, their failure so far to find any hint of where Dawn was seemed like the type of nightmare a person wakes up gasping and sweating from. But this wasn't a dream. It was reality. Where the hell was she? As he stepped out of the truck, Ted said a silent prayer that his daughter would be at the Reese house.

"I drove over to the Reese house," Ted said. "It was kind of late. Paul Reese, the father, wasn't there. The mother, Barbara Reese, a couple of her sons, and the youngest Reese daughter were there. I told the mother that I had heard that Dawn was over there, and she told me that, no, she hadn't seen Dawn that day. I insisted that several people had told us that Dawn had been there. The little girl, she couldn't have been more than five or six, spoke up and said, 'Mommy, Dawn was here . . .' The mother whirled around and slapped the little girl really hard across the mouth."

As Ted witnessed this act, it both stunned him and made it blatantly obvious to him that his daughter *had* been there, and that Barbara Reese was lying for some reason. Why else would she slap the little girl? He knew that there was no way he was just going to leave. This was the closest thing to a clue they'd gotten so far about where Dawn might have gone that day.

"When the mother smacked the little girl in the mouth, that pretty much told me they had something to hide," Ted recalled. "You just don't smack a child as hard as you can unless you're really scared of what she might say."

Ted, now overcome with a sick dread, wouldn't let Barbara close the door. Something was wrong. He just knew it. He insisted that he be allowed to come inside and see for himself that Dawn wasn't there. Barbara, though at first reluctant, finally said fine, come on in. She still insisted that Dawn wasn't there, though, and that she hadn't seen her that day. Ted, Wesley, and Michelle stepped inside before Barbara could change her mind.

"When I was over there trying to find my daughter they were very deceptive about everything," Ted would later tell the news media. "It was obvious to me they weren't being truthful from their actions and the glances between them."

When Ted walked into the Reese home, he couldn't believe its condition. "Practically every space in the house was covered with piles of junk," he recalled. Never in his life, Ted would later say, had he seen such a cramped, cluttered house. The family had what looked like trash stacked and piled everywhere. Ted made his way along the paths that wound through the stacks on the first floor of the house, calling out Dawn's name over and over. Next, he looked around in the garage, also packed with junk, once more calling out his daughter's name. The garage, however, had no electricity, and Ted hadn't brought along a flashlight, so he couldn't really do much of a search. Finally, Ted went down into the basement, where he saw a pool table—and more piles of junk stacked everywhere. They could have hidden an elephant down there, he thought, and no one would have seen it.

Like his nephew Wesley, Ted also said that something about the basement disturbed him. It gave him an uncomfortable, queasy feeling.

"I really didn't feel comfortable in the house. I went down into the basement, but there was so much stuff stacked around that I couldn't do a thorough search. I had a really bad feeling while I was in the house. The hair on the back of my neck stood up." Ted looked around in the basement as best he could and called out Dawn's name over and over, but to no avail.

He left the Reese house reluctantly, feeling that something was very wrong there. But he didn't know what else he could do. Barbara Reese had let him come in to search, but Ted hadn't found anything that showed Dawn had been there. Wesley told Ted about following a visitor to the Reese house back to an apartment, so Wesley and Ted drove to the apartment and again talked to Timothy Keller. Timothy still denied knowing anything, and took them to another person who knew the Reeses, but he couldn't give them much information. Finally, Timothy went with Ted and Wesley back to the Reese house, but Ted still couldn't find out anything about Dawn. Frustrated and now in real fear for his daughter, Ted went back home, where he and his wife Sandy tried to figure out if there was any place they hadn't yet looked for Dawn.

Ted and Sandy began double-checking all of the places their daughter might have gone to. They rechecked the church, the school playground, and all of Dawn's friends' houses. They asked every person they met about whether he or she had seen their daughter, but no one had, and it soon became too late to wake up people they had already spoken to just to ask them again if they knew where Dawn might be.

After realizing that there was nowhere else to look, they finally decided it was time to call the police. Like many parents of missing children, Ted and Sandy hadn't wanted to involve the police until they realized they likely weren't going to find their daughter on their own.

However, when Ted and Sandy went to the local police substation to file a missing person report, they were told that a report couldn't be taken until Dawn had been missing for twenty-four hours. That was standard policy in 1986, but still Ted simply couldn't believe it. A young, innocent little girl was missing, and this officer was telling him that the police couldn't be bothered to look for her until the next day? That was unbelievable! Who knew what could happen to her in that time? Ted was furious.

The officer was sympathetic and offered a solution: If, rather than filing a missing person report, Ted and Sandy filed a runaway complaint, the police could start looking for Dawn right away. Ted knew that there was absolutely no way that his daughter would have run away from home. She was a good kid who had never given him or her mother even the smallest sign that she was unhappy. As a matter of fact, he thought, Dawn was the happiest little girl he had ever known. Ted and Sandy stood there for several moments, not knowing what to do. They didn't want to give their daughter a police record as a runaway, but they also knew they needed the police to help them look for Dawn. They finally decided that they could work out the runaway problem later. So just before 1:00 A.M. on March 17, 1986, Sandy Stuard signed a complaint saying that she believed her daughter Dawn was a runaway.

After receiving assurances that the police would now

join in their search for Dawn (which they did, including several officers who searched the Reese house themselves), Ted and Sandy then went back to trying to figure out where their daughter might be. After his uncomfortable visit there, Ted still felt certain that Dawn must've been in the Reese house for at least a little while earlier that day. The little girl who had gotten slapped had very likely been telling the truth. But Dawn certainly wasn't there now, or the mother wouldn't have allowed him to come in and look around. But why would Barbara Reese lie about her having been there earlier—and where could Dawn be now?

And so, even though Ted and Sandy knew that the police were now out looking, too, the longest and most horrible night of their lives passed. Unable to sleep, they continued to search their neighborhood, while at the same time always hoping to hear from the police or perhaps from one of the many people they had contacted. They desperately wanted someone to call with news of where Dawn was. But the night dragged on and on without any such call. With every passing minute, the fear and dread that had now settled on them like a suffocating black mist became more intense. They circled around again and again to places they had already checked. Who knew, they told each other, she might still show up at one of those places. They also decided to investigate these places more thoroughly. Dawn could have been injured and was lying unconscious somewhere out of sight.

As they continued their search, Ted and Sandy turned their minds against the worst-case scenarios of what

might have happened. Most parents won't allow themselves to think about these. Instead, frightened parents
try to think of other possibilities. At any moment, they
believe, their child will turn up, having just gotten lost
or maybe having stayed too late at a friend's house. Or
perhaps the child is lying injured and unconscious at the
one hospital or clinic they hadn't called. Or maybe the
child is a runaway after all. Maybe the child just wants to
be rebellious and has run away but will return before
long. These are the kind of thoughts that will allow the
parents of a good child who has disappeared to keep
their sanity. To think about or even consider the other
possibilities, many parents believe, would almost certainly bring on insanity.

Ted knew that if Dawn had actually run away or had
gone to some friend's house they hadn't visited, that as a
parent he should be angry when he finally found her, and
that he might even try to act that way for her. But in reality, he knew that he would want to hug and kiss her, and
to hold her in his arms and tell her how important she
was to him and Sandy, and how much they loved her.

Later that Monday morning, March 17, 1986, Ted
checked back in with the police. Had they found out
anything? They had not. So Ted and Sandy continued
revisiting every location they could think of where Dawn
might be. They again checked with their neighbors,
Dawn's friends, all of the nearby businesses, teen hangouts, Dawn's school. But no one had seen her.

At a little after 1:30 that afternoon, Sandy received

some extremely unsettling news. A friend who had a police scanner called to tell her that she'd heard a police call go out over the scanner saying a woman had reported finding a body in the 4600 block of East 23rd Street, about a mile north of Ted and Sandy's house. When Sandy told Ted the news, his heart felt as if it had suddenly turned to granite and simply dropped loose in his chest.

As he and Sandy got into their truck and raced toward the East 23rd Street address, Ted kept telling himself over and over that it didn't mean anything. The police probably found bodies all the time. The body could be a drug killing just dumped there, or it could be a homeless person who had died while camped out there. It couldn't be Dawn. His mind simply wouldn't consider it. His daughter was still going to show up. He was just sure of it.

Still, a deadly cold had settled over him, though he tried to shrug it off. At 4600 East 23rd Street, an area where only a few homes bordered a wooded section that ran along a little creek called Pogue's Run, Ted parked his truck next to several Indianapolis Police Department cars. Nearby, he saw a couple of obviously unmarked police cars also parked there. The area, he noticed as he and Sandy got out of their truck, had what looked like rope wrapped around a number of trees and an unmarked police car, closing off an area on a steep hill that ran down to the water. Several grim-faced uniformed police officers stood guard just outside the barrier. Ted could see that inside the roped-off area two men in suits were bending over what he supposed was the body they had discovered, but, because the hill was so steep, he couldn't see anything else from where he was.

Ted approached one of the uniformed officers and gave him his name, and told him that he had a daughter who was missing. The uniformed officer told Ted that the detectives were busy but that he would convey Ted's information to them, and that he was certain they would want to speak with him. So Ted stepped back and waited. He'd already convinced himself on the trip over there that there was no way this body could be his daughter, so he started feeling a little guilty about wasting time just standing around when he and Sandy should be out looking for Dawn. Still, he watched anxiously as the detectives seemed to move in slow motion, and became particularly anxious when one of the detectives elected to give a press interview before coming over to talk to him.

"I was just standing there trying to see what was going on," Ted recalled. "We had to just stand there and wait as the detective gave an interview to the press."

Like the previous evening at the police substation, Ted wanted to scream in frustration, but he knew that the detectives were just doing their jobs. And so, since there was nothing else they could do, Ted and Sandy Stuard had no choice but to simply wait.

TWO

Detective Sergeant Roy West sat in the Homicide Office of the Indianapolis Police Department on St. Patrick's Day, March 17, 1986. The Homicide Office, located on the fourth floor of the six-story police headquarters at 50 North Alabama Street, was the ultimate assignment for any detective. It was the assignment most detectives strove for and dreamed about. Being assigned to the Homicide Branch meant that the detective was the best of the best. Being assigned there meant that the detective was part of the elite.

But there was no easy route or straight shot to the position. A police officer first had to demonstrate exceptional ability as an investigator, and it often took officers years to work their way through lesser detective jobs before getting an assignment to the Homicide Branch. And once they did earn the assignment, the hard work was far from over. Being a homicide detective wasn't merely an eight-hour-a-day job. It required working long, long hours until a case was either solved or every lead had been exhausted. It meant sticking with a case until there were no more clues to be investigated, staying sixteen to eighteen hours a day on the job, grabbing a couple hours of sleep, and then coming back for another sixteen- to eighteen-hour stint. New homicide detectives were under a lot of pressure to prove themselves worthy of the assignment. Therefore, their first few cases could be extremely stressful.

On that March 17, 1986, Detective West, a fourteen-year veteran of the police department, had been assigned to the Homicide Branch for less than two months. He'd transferred there after serving nearly three years as a narcotics detective. West had quickly discovered that homicide investigation differed drastically from narcotics investigation, not just in the long hours the job required, but more particularly when it came to the victims. Practically everyone West had dealt with in narcotics investigations had broken the law by being involved somehow in the illegal drug trade, either as a user or a seller. He had encountered very few guiltless individuals as a narcotics detective. But in a homicide, the victim could indeed be totally innocent. Certainly, some homicide victims were involved in illegal or violent situations, where their less-than-blameless lifestyles pointed to a motive and possible suspect. But there were also cases where the victims did nothing at all to bring about the fates they suffered.

Although West had been excited for the chance to

work as a homicide detective, having at last attained a position so many others coveted, he'd also been extremely anxious and nervous the last few days, waiting for the next homicide call to come in. With homicide cases, the detectives worked as teams, assisting one another with the various tasks that needed to be completed. In each investigation, though, one person would be designated the lead detective, the one ultimately responsible for the case. Since West was new to the Homicide Office, he had not yet been assigned a case as lead detective, but now it was time. West had been put into the case rotation. He knew that the homicide commander had decided the next case that came in on West's shift would become his case to investigate. West's chest filled with electricity and his stomach pulled into sickening knots every time a police radio broadcast came out or the main telephone in the office rang.

Up until now, West had just been assisting other homicide detectives as they worked their cases, trying to pick up the nuances of the job. And the job, West quickly discovered, was extremely complex, with dozens of details that had to be taken care of, each one crucial to the success of a case. Not a single detail could be overlooked.

The man West had been partnered with, veteran homicide detective Tom Minor, had been very patient with him and had tried to give West the benefit of his years of experience as a homicide detective. Still, West felt jumpy and nervous. Screwing up a narcotics investigation by forgetting some detail mainly only affected his pride. The worst that could happen with a bungled narcotics case was that the perpetrators would be cut free, but they would almost always be back committing crimes immediately and so could usually be arrested again fairly easily. But screwing up a homicide investigation could have monumental and disastrous results, not only to a detective's career, but more importantly to the victims and their families. Screwing up a homicide investigation could mean that a murderer would walk free, and that justice would be denied forever to the victim. There was a belief held by all of the detectives in the Homicide Office that since murder victims couldn't speak for themselves, homicide detectives spoke for them. They were the victim's voice, one that demanded justice. And no homicide detective wanted to fail the victims he or she spoke for.

At around 1:30 in the afternoon of March 17, 1986, the call West had anxiously been waiting for finally came in. The body of a possible murder victim had been found.

According to the report West received, a woman named Kathleen Rueter had called the police a few minutes earlier. She told the dispatcher that while walking her daughter to school after lunch, she had spotted a body lying on a small hill in the 4600 block of East 23rd Street. Mrs. Rueter said that she hadn't wanted to alarm or traumatize her daughter, so she took her on to school before calling the police.

West and his partner, Detective Tom Minor, put on their suit jackets, grabbed their notebooks, and left the office. They took the elevator (which seemed to West to travel extra slow that day) down to their car. West felt like he should be running but knew that it wouldn't have looked professional. Since uniformed officers would quickly secure the incident scene and then guard it against intrusion, there was really no reason for homicide detectives to run or even to drive with their flashing lights and siren on (as was often shown in the movies or on TV, for dramatic effect). But still, West didn't want to waste any time getting to the possible crime scene.

In 1986, the neighborhood they were headed to was a sparsely populated area of Indianapolis, mostly woods that ran along a small creek named after early Indianapolis settler George Pogue. Although largely an underground stream, Pogue's Run in the 4600 block of East 23rd Street babbled along aboveground, only a foot or less deep in most areas.

When West and Minor arrived, they found that, as protocol and police department policy demanded, the scene where the body had been discovered had been marked off with rope. The officers had wrapped the rope around a police car and around numerous trees in the area. Several uniformed officers stood just outside the rope, guarding the incident scene against unauthorized entry. West was glad to see that, because a guarded, uncontaminated crime scene can often make the difference as to whether a murder case is solved or not.

Although it would seem logical for detectives to immediately go into the cordoned-off area and head for the body at a homicide crime scene (as is often depicted in books and movies), there are other matters that must be taken care of first. In most homicides, detectives find the best and most damning evidence at the crime scene. Therefore, the crime scene has to be properly and carefully processed, beginning with a thorough documentation of the scene by crime scene technicians. Fortunately for Detective Sergeant Roy West, the scene on East 23rd Street didn't appear to be overly disturbed or to have attracted an exorbitant amount of outside attention. The uniformed police officers, after assuring that the scene was safe and no witnesses were nearby, had quickly cordoned off the area and protected it until West arrived.

The weather on March 17, 1986, was cloudy and relatively warm, low fifties, with no snow on the ground (as occasionally could be the case in Indiana at that time of year). West was relieved not to have to worry about any evidence on the ground being hidden by the snow and consequently hard to find. On the other hand, no snow meant no tracks in the snow from the perpetrator coming into or leaving the crime scene.

While the crime scene technician was photographing and videotaping the crime scene, Detective West spoke with the first responding uniformed officer. This would give him a clear picture of what the officer saw when he'd initially responded, and of any changes that had occurred to the crime scene since then. The first responding officer had been Patrolman Jeremiah Sedam. He made the original report, which the police department designated case number 296589F. Following this, West performed an initial walk-through of the crime scene on East 23rd Street. The body lay on a steep slope, and there appeared to be a footprint from someone who'd slipped

at the start of the steep slope. That would be photo-
graphed and preserved. West also spied several pieces of
the *Indianapolis Star*, the city's morning newspaper, on
the ground close to the body. The pieces appeared to
have blue and black spray paint marks on them, as though
someone had spray-painted something that had been sitting on the papers.

Since the ground around where the victim lay contained scant evidence and also appeared mostly undis-
turbed, West's immediate tentative theory was that the
victim had likely been killed elsewhere and then brought
there and dumped. The perpetrator, he surmised, had
stopped a vehicle on the nearby road, carried the body
down to this site, dumped it, and then walked back to
the vehicle and left.

After marking the pieces of newspaper as evidence for
the crime scene technicians to recover, West finally
walked over and examined the body. He found the victim to be a young, white female with blond hair. He
guessed her to be between four feet ten and four feet
eleven (she would later be found to be actually five feet
two and weighed 119 pounds) and between twelve and
fourteen years of age. She was lying facedown on the side
of a steep hill, surrounded by discarded tires, old lumber,
chunks of concrete, and other trash. The area, it appeared, was an illegal dumping site. West noted that the
girl wore blue jeans, a blouse, brown deck shoes, and a
lavender jacket. West could see small green and gold fibers, later identified as carpet fibers, in the victim's hair
and on her clothing. He also saw several small pieces of

carpeting near her. When the deputy coroner arrived, West made certain to point out the fibers to him so that they wouldn't be lost when the body was transferred to the morgue for an autopsy.

Of course the deputy coroner, in his own examination, likely would have known to note and remove those carpet fibers and place them in evidence envelopes, but West needed to be certain it was done. Since he was new to homicide, West wasn't yet familiar with the deputy coroner (in this case, Dr. Dean Hawley). In Indiana, the coroner is an elected official who isn't required to have any medical training at all, nor are any of his or her deputy coroners (though many, such as Dr. Hawley, do). West knew that the competence of a coroner could mean the difference between a successful murder investigation and a failure, since much of the information a homicide detective uses in his or her investigation comes from the coroner.

The coroner's job at a homicide crime scene is not to determine the official cause of death (that will be determined later at the autopsy) but to examine the body for injuries (including defensive wounds, which are wounds sustained trying to ward off an attack); to look for any evidence on the body, such as blood, saliva, semen, fibers, and so forth; and to determine if it appears the body has been the victim of foul play. On East 23rd Street, it was determined that this did indeed appear to be the case with the young girl. During the examination of her body, Dr. Hawley noted some blunt force trauma to the victim's head and neck, and possible evidence of strangulation. He estimated that the girl had been dead a little less than twenty-four hours. This was as close a determination as he could make in the field. Following his initial examination, the deputy coroner then had the young girl's body placed into a body bag and called for a stretcher to carry her to the waiting transport vehicle.

Meanwhile, Ted and Sandy Stuard, who stood outside the crime scene, felt as if they were having a waking nightmare. At this point, they had been waiting around for what seemed to them to be hours to talk to a detective about their missing daughter, Dawn, and although they might not have been aware of it, the uniformed officer who had talked to them had been watching them carefully.

The first uniformed officers responding to the scene of a murder and those guarding the perimeter of the crime scene always want to quickly identify and closely watch any possible family members of a victim. They need to do this for several reasons. Often, these individuals will know something important about the crime; occasionally, they are involved in the crime. Also, it's not uncommon for family members to crash through a crime scene barrier and run up to hug the body, unable to comprehend what has happened. While understandable, naturally those actions can do untold damage to the crime scene. Obscuring the identity of the victim from onlookers is one of several reasons police officers are trained to extend the perimeter of a crime scene farther than the actual scene.

In this case, Ted Stuard had tried to see what was going on inside the crime scene but couldn't see the victim. And so he and his wife Sandy just stood and waited for a detective to come and speak with them.

Before walking over to the Stuards, Detective West gave a statement to the news media, with the hope that someone who saw the news report would know who his victim was. He would later say that he hadn't known someone who could possibly identify the victim was already at the scene. When Detective Sergeant West finally did come over to speak with Ted and Sandy Stuard and learned the details of Dawn's disappearance, along with her description, however, he knew that Dawn was very likely his victim. But he didn't say so to the Stuards—there was still a minute possibility that he could be wrong, and he did not want to unnecessarily traumatize the parents until he was certain that the victim was Dawn Stuard. West questioned Ted and Sandy with as much compassion and sympathy, but also with as much thoroughness, as he could. While it is understandably hard for close relatives of a possible murder victim to think clearly at such times, it still is the best time to get the most accurate information; before family members can forget key facts, and also before they have time to talk with others about what has happened and allow other people's perceptions to color their own.

Ted told West everything he knew—how he and his wife had left town for Ohio on Sunday, how their daughter, Dawn, hadn't shown up at her aunt's house, and how, after the aunt called him, he and his wife had hurried home. He then told West about how he and his wife had checked everywhere in the neighborhood looking for their daughter. Ted also mentioned how suspicious the Reese family had acted.

Once West had collected all of the information he felt he could get from Ted and Sandy Stuard at that time, he was reasonably sure that his victim was indeed the Stuards' missing daughter. He then had to have Ted conduct an even more difficult task—the body identification. West took Ted over to the waiting transport vehicle, where the victim's body had been placed, and asked him to look and see if the person they'd found that morning was his daughter.

This is naturally a very traumatic and horrifying thing for a family member to have to do, and even the most hardened homicide detective will be affected by it. But it has to be done. Confirming the identity of a murder victim is extremely important for a homicide investigation. Knowing the victim's identity gives the homicide detective a place to start in the investigation. Knowing who the victim is, the homicide detective can then trace the victim's movements, learn about the possible motives for the murder, determine who last saw the victim alive, and find people who knew the victim well enough to give the homicide detective the information he or she needs to conduct the investigation.

And so, West stood by quietly with Ted Stuard and waited as the driver of the transport vehicle unzipped the bag. When the body came into view, the nightmare Ted had been avoiding became horrifyingly real. With tears now blurring his vision, he nodded.

It was Dawn.

Words couldn't really describe the feeling of that horrible moment. "The hardest thing I've ever done is identify my daughter," Ted told the news media later. "Your whole world just crashes right there."

After the body identification, the deputy coroner left with the body, and the Stuards went home. Detective West then carefully examined the entire crime scene for a second time, and would even eventually come back for a third search. He discovered more carpet fibers on the ground leading away from where the body had been found and heading up to the road, which supported his theory that Dawn had been killed somewhere else and then dumped, a not uncommon occurrence in homicides. But along with this follow-up search, Detective West had also set up a canvass of the surrounding area, which meant having detectives knock on every door for several blocks around the murder scene to ask the residents if they knew anything about the murder or the victim. A neighborhood canvass can become a crucial part of any homicide investigation, as detectives often find people who have witnessed something important to a murder case, something they didn't realize the significance of at the time. Also, some people with important information won't contact the police for fear of being labeled as a snitch but will talk if an officer comes to their door. A canvass will usually be repeated more than once, to ensure that detectives reach everyone who may not have been at home during the previous canvasses.

In the canvass around the East 23rd Street site, detectives found several witnesses who said that their dogs had begun barking quite vigorously around 1:30 that morning, but since the area had no street lights, they hadn't been able to see what the dogs were barking at. They assumed it was just some wild animal.

This being his first case, and wanting very much to succeed as a homicide detective, West became committed to doing the absolute best job possible to bring this homicide investigation to a successful conclusion. Nothing, he told himself, would escape his search. He would not let his first case go unsolved. He had a very young girl as a victim, much too young to have been involved in most of the situations that usually lead to murder. *What could she have done to deserve such a death?* he wondered.

"This was a truly innocent victim," West said about his first impressions of the case.

And so, after finishing at the crime scene, West then began the next step in the investigation of a murder— developing suspects. He knew he had a starting point from his interview with the Stuards: the Reese family.

THREE

Detective Sergeant Roy West, after giving the crime scene on East 23rd Street as thorough a follow-up search as he could, finally left the area late in the afternoon of March 17, 1986. Working with information he had received from the Stuards and from several of the officers he spoke with who had been involved in the search for Dawn the previous day, he drove over to the Reese house at 1428 North Bosart Street. West had found out that after Ted and Sandy Stuard had reported Dawn as a runaway, the officers had conducted an extremely thorough search for the girl, including stopping at the Reese house and questioning the occupants about Dawn.

But that was when Dawn Stuard was merely missing, before they knew that she was dead, and likely murdered. Now West wanted to take the investigation to the next level. He had the occupants of the Reese house transported downtown to the Homicide Office for interviews.

West knew it was very possible that one of these people could be Dawn's killer or a witness to her death, so he took the Reeses down to the Homicide Office because he wanted to question them somewhere out of their comfort zone. When people are in locations where they feel comfortable, they are more likely to be able to resist the interviewer's attempt to extract information from them that they don't want to tell. West knew he'd be asking some tough questions, and he wanted to do it in a location where he was in control. The interview rooms at police headquarters were closed-off rooms with no distractions and nothing for the interviewees to look at other than the police officer questioning them. Inside the interview rooms were only the beige metal walls and gray metal furniture. No pictures, no computers, no decorations. And while one might think that police officers would have difficulty getting people to agree to questioning, actually the opposite is true. Individuals who are innocent typically want to help police get the matter cleared up—and guilty individuals usually want to look innocent, so they also tend to readily agree to go to police headquarters for questioning.

Paul Reese Sr., though, hadn't been at the house on North Bosart Street with the others. However, West found out that he had been calling the Bosart Street house from Crawford's Tavern on South Meridian Street, so he had sent some officers there to pick him up. Sure enough, the officers found him there, and while Paul Sr.

at first gave the officers a phony name, he eventually did go with them.

As he drove downtown to conduct the interviews, West stayed busy trying to formulate his questions. Initial interviews are usually meant to elicit information that will point the homicide detective in the direction of a suspect. They seldom solve a homicide, but they do often give a detective a starting point for the investigation, and if conducted properly, they can often offer the detective a motive and can point to the location of other evidence or possibly even a suspect. While physical evidence can often play a more crucial role than witness testimony, witness statements are still valuable. Fortunately, Detective West had honed his interview skills while working in narcotics. Narcotics abusers are some of the biggest liars police officers ever encounter. Finally, at a little after 6:00 P.M. on March 17, 1986, West was ready to begin the interviews.

The first person he spoke with was Paul Reese Sr., the forty-three-year-old father of the family. Paul Sr. told West that since Barbara had filed for divorce he didn't live full-time at the house on North Bosart Street, though when he did stay there he helped around the house by doing maintenance and other work. Otherwise, he said, he lived with his own father. "I stay with my dad at his house on Lake Road a lot," he told West. "I just kind of drift back and forth between the two houses."

Paul Sr. went on to explain that he and his wife had gone through divorce proceedings in 1979, but that he wasn't sure if the divorce had ever been finalized because he had never paid his attorney. Regardless, Paul Sr. said, he and Barbara had never really tried to get back together, in part because he could never get a good job, and wasn't employed at the moment.

When asked about the events of March 16, 1986, Paul Sr. said that around 10:00 A.M. a seventeen-year-old named Timothy Joe Keller had knocked on the door and said that he and Paul Sr.'s sixteen-year-old son, Paul Reese Jr., were supposed to go sell some things at the Liberty Bell Flea Market on the west side of Indianapolis. (West would later learn that the things the boys were selling were items they had stolen from neighbors' yards; they were taking them to a flea market all the way across town in the hopes that no one there would recognize the stolen goods.) Paul Sr. told West that he let Timothy in, and then about ten minutes later, Dawn Stuard had also knocked on the back door and Timothy let her in. Dawn told them that she was there because she was supposed to help Barbara Reese collect payments on her paper route that day. Paul Sr. said he didn't know why the thirteen-year-old girl was there so early, since Barbara never got up until late in the afternoon, after her early morning paper delivery. Dawn asked Paul Sr. if he wanted to play pool. He said he would in a little while.

Dawn took a seat at the table and everybody just sat there talking for a while until Paul Jr. and Pam Winningham (Paul Jr.'s seventeen-year-old girlfriend who lived in the basement with him) woke up and got ready to go. "It was probably a half hour or so," Paul Sr. said. Then Timothy, Paul Jr., and Pam left in Timothy's white Ford

Pinto to pick up the items that they hoped to sell that day at the flea market. Dawn stayed at the house with Paul Sr. There were others in the house, but they were asleep.

There was a pool table in the basement, and Paul Sr. went on to say that Dawn again said she wanted to play pool, so the two of them went downstairs. "She wanted to shoot a game of pool," Paul Sr. told West, "and so I shot her a game until they came back." About fifteen minutes after Paul Sr. and Dawn went down into the basement, Timothy, Pam, and Paul Jr. returned.

At about this same time, Pam's father, Carvel Winningham, who went by the nickname of "Cotton," pulled up in his black Chevrolet Chevette out front. Pam went out to the car and she and Cotton argued for a bit about a court hearing scheduled for the next day, but they finally left together. When Paul Sr. told his son that he'd seen Pam and her father fighting, Paul Jr. and Timothy ran out and followed Pam and her father for a while in Tim's car to be sure that Pam was all right. They followed Pam and her father to a McDonald's at East 10th Street and North Bosart, saw that everything seemed okay between them, and then came back.

After that, Paul Sr. said, the guys left to go to the flea market, and he and Dawn played a couple more games of pool in the basement. Paul Sr. said that Dawn stayed for an hour or two. While they were down in the basement playing pool, another friend of Paul Jr.'s, a sixteen-year-old named Doyle Stinson, knocked on the door. When Paul Sr. saw who it was, he sent Dawn upstairs to tell

Doyle that Paul Jr. wasn't there. Paul Sr. said that he didn't want to talk to Doyle himself.

When West asked how long Dawn stayed at the house, Paul Sr. answered, "Oh gosh, I don't know, probably an hour or two, something like that." He then added that he thought she left at around noon.

Detective West pressed for more details, and Paul Sr. said that Dawn had been coming around for about a year, helping Barbara with the paper route. He said that, along with being a friend of his daughter Jenny, Dawn also came over to see two of his other sons, Jeremy and Johnny (before they were incarcerated at the Juvenile Detention Center). Paul Sr. first told West that he stayed at the house on North Bosart Street all day that Sunday, March 16, but then corrected himself and said he drove around a bit with Timothy Keller later that evening. Paul Sr. told West that the two of them drove around for a couple of hours, from around 8:00 to 10:00 P.M., but didn't go anywhere in particular.

West asked Paul Sr. what he and Dawn had talked about in the basement. "Dawn and I didn't talk about nothing really," he said. "There wasn't really much to talk about. She liked to shoot pool, and me and her had shot the day before. I was about five games up on her and she was trying to catch up."

Paul Reese Sr. insisted to Detective West that after Dawn left the house around noon, he hadn't seen her again, and said that Barbara had wondered why Dawn didn't come back later to go on the paper route with her.

Continuing his story, Paul Sr. said that Timothy dropped him off at the house on North Bosart at around 10:00 P.M., then Paul Sr. went inside and got a cup of coffee. Shortly after that, Dawn's parents showed up and asked if anyone knew where she was. He then corrected himself again and told Detective West that Dawn's parents had also been at the house just before he'd first left to go drive around with Timothy. Paul Sr. said that he hadn't talked with them, but that his wife and girls did. He added that he heard Barbara had let Dawn's father come into the house and look around, but that he had never personally met the Stuards. Paul Sr. then told West that the second time Dawn's parents showed up, they said they were going to have the police search the house, and, shortly after this, one of his daughters came in and told him he'd better get out of there, so he left again. When asked why, Paul Sr. said that it was because they had a warrant out on him for a back child support charge, and he didn't want to go to jail.

When asked where he had gone after leaving the house at 10:00 P.M., Paul Sr. said that he went over to the apartments where Timothy Keller lived, in the 1900 block of North Wallace Avenue, but that when the police showed up there (apparently investigating some stolen bicycles) he quickly left and went to the home of Jay Ward, another friend of his son's. Paul Sr. then borrowed a bicycle from his son's friend, and just as he did, the police pulled up to Ward's house, so he got on the bicycle and pedaled by the house at 1428 North Bosart Street, but saw police cars everywhere. And so, Paul Sr. said, he just rode the bicycle around until the police finally left the North Bosart Street area, and then he went back inside the house.

Paul Sr. told West that as he sat in the house, drinking more coffee, the police would drive by every fifteen minutes or so. Barbara had gone on to bed, but Paul Sr. said that he sat there until she got up at about 3:00 A.M. to deliver the morning newspaper and that he went with her. He said Barbara told him that something bad had happened in the neighborhood and that's why the police were everywhere. But Dawn Stuard's name, he claimed, didn't come up.

"I didn't hear from Dawn after she left the house around noon," he insisted again. "I haven't seen her since she left." When asked, he emphatically denied having anything to do with Dawn's death.

West didn't believe a lot of the man's story. Paul Sr. seemed skittish and had given far too many signs that he wasn't telling the truth. But West also knew that this early in the investigation, he had nothing really substantial to confront Paul Reese Sr. with in the hope that he would come clean. West hoped that would happen later, after the investigation had progressed a bit further.

After Detective West finished interviewing Paul Reese Sr., he then spoke with Paul Reese Jr. The teenager said that he'd known Dawn Stuard for a year or two, and that she'd been at his house on March 16, 1986. Paul Jr. told West that Dawn came over all the time to see the family because she was good friends with them.

"I saw Dawn yesterday," he told Detective West. "She

was at our house between 10:00 and 11:30. She sat and talked with me and Dad and everyone."

Paul Jr. said that they'd all sat at the kitchen table Sunday morning and chatted before he, Pam, and Timothy Keller left to get the items they planned to sell that day at a flea market. When they came back, Pam left with her father, and he and Timothy went to the flea market. He said that this was at around 11:30 A.M. Dawn, he added, was still there when he and Timothy left. He said that his mother Barbara was asleep in her room the whole time, and he didn't see her at all that morning.

Paul Jr. went on to say that when he got home from the flea market later that night at around 6:30 P.M., his mom and dad were both home, along with Pam and his sisters. He said they all watched television and that his father left sometime around 10:00 P.M., about ten minutes before the police showed up. (He didn't say anything about the earlier visits from Wesley Collins or the Stuards.) No one, he told West, mentioned Dawn that evening. The next day, however, on March 17, 1986, Paul Jr. said that at around 10:30 A.M. Timothy Keller and a guy he didn't know came knocking on the door. Apparently, the police who'd been investigating Dawn as a runaway had spoken with Timothy Keller; Paul Jr. said that Timothy, who was visibly shaken, and the other guy began asking him all kinds of questions about Dawn that apparently the police had asked them, like how well he knew her, if she had been there at his house, and if he knew where she was. They also asked him if he knew where his dad was. Timothy obviously hadn't liked the police coming to his house to question him. Paul Jr. told them that he didn't know anything about Dawn and that he didn't know where his dad was, either.

West concluded his interview with Paul Reese Jr. but figured that he would have much more to ask later.

Homicide detective Tom Minor, acting as assistant in this case, interviewed the mother of the family, Barbara Reese. She told Minor that she had six children living with her on Bosart Street, her four sons: Paul Jr., John, Brian, and Jeremy; and her two daughters: Jenny and Cindy. Barbara then added that Pam Winningham also lived there with Paul Jr. but told Minor that her ex-husband, Paul Reese Sr., didn't live there.

"I'm not actually employed myself," she told Detective Minor. "I help my kids with their newspaper routes. And as for Paul Sr.," she added, "I don't know where he lives."

When Detective Minor asked her about Dawn Stuard, Barbara told him that she had known Dawn for about three years, and that the last time she'd seen her was two days earlier, on Saturday, March 15, 1986, when Dawn had helped her and her two daughters deliver inserts to the newspaper. At around 7:00 P.M. that Saturday, Barbara said, Dawn told her that she had to be home before dark and got out of Barbara's car while on the paper route and started walking home. That was the last time she had seen the girl.

Minor asked Barbara for more details about the paper routes. She said that she had woken up around 5:30 A.M. on Sunday, March 16, and drove her car to deliver the newspapers. She gave Minor the boundaries of the four routes she delivered on, and he made a note that the routes were very close to the area where Dawn's body had been found.

Detective Minor then asked Barbara about the events of March 16, 1986, specifically what happened after she delivered the Sunday newspapers and returned home. Barbara said that she arrived home at around 9:00 A.M. and went back to bed. She added that her ex-husband must have come over while she was sleeping, because at around 11:00 A.M. he came into her bedroom, as he often did, and asked her what time she wanted him to get her up. Barbara told him to wake her at around 2:00 or 3:00 P.M. and then went back to sleep. When she got up later on, Barbara said, she, Pam, and her two daughters went to AMVETS, a secondhand store, and returned home at around 6:00 P.M. Her son Paul Jr. returned home from the flea market shortly after that, then around 6:30 P.M., she, her ex-husband, and their two daughters went to collect payment on the paper routes. They returned around 8:30 P.M. and all watched television. Paul Sr., she said, left the house on foot between 10:00 and 10:30 P.M.

When asked about Dawn Stuard, Barbara said that her ex-husband told her Dawn had been there that morning, but that the girl left between 11:00 A.M. and noon. Barbara hadn't seen Dawn herself that day because she was asleep. Dawn's parents, Barbara told Detective Minor, showed up at her home on North Bosart between 10:30 and 11:00 P.M., right after her ex-husband had left, and the police came by just a little after that. (Although these times didn't seem right, inaccuracies like this always occur when taking statements, and Minor knew that West would have to straighten them out later.) Barbara said that she let Dawn's father come in and look around the house, and later that night, a policeman also went through the house. Detective Minor thanked her and concluded the interview, knowing that West would want to follow up with Barbara Reese at another time.

Detective Minor then spoke with seventeen-year-old Pam Winningham, who told Minor that she had met Dawn Stuard about three times, all at the Reese house. She told Minor that she didn't know Dawn well because she had only been living there with Paul Jr. for about six weeks, but that the girl would come over to play pool at the house and help Barbara on the paper routes. At around 9:30 A.M. on March 16, 1986, Pam claimed, Timothy Keller arrived and woke her and Paul Jr. up.

"When I went upstairs," Pam told Detective Minor, "Dawn was sitting at the kitchen table with Paul Sr. Dawn asked me if I wanted to play some pool, but I told her I couldn't. I had to go with Paul Jr. and Timothy to pick up some things to take to the flea market."

The three of them then left, Pam said, at around 10:30 A.M. in Timothy's white Ford Pinto, which had several lawn mowers in back. They returned around 11:00 A.M., which was when Pam found her father waiting in his car out front. She got into the car with him and left.

Pam said her father brought her back to the Reese house at around 4:30 P.M. but he didn't come in, because he wasn't friends with Paul Reese Sr. She told Detective Minor that Paul Sr., Barbara, and the two Reese daughters, Jenny and Cindy, were all there when she returned, but that Paul Jr. was still at the flea market. She said it appeared that Paul Sr. had just taken a shower. Pam went on to say that she talked with the two Reese girls for a while and that Jenny told her Dawn had gone home but had been expected to come back around 4:00 P.M. Jenny didn't say where she got this information. At around 6:30 P.M., Paul Jr. returned home from the flea market, and Pam added that at around 7:30 P.M. the two of them went down to the room they shared in the basement and went to sleep for a while.

At around 10:30 P.M., however, Pam said that she and Paul Jr. got up and went out, walking a few streets over to check out a car someone had for sale. When they returned, Pam said that Dawn Stuard's aunt, cousin, and parents were there. (She wasn't quite right—it was actually Dawn's father, Ted Stuard; her cousin Wesley Collins; and Wesley's girlfriend Michelle Lynch.) Pam said the Stuards wanted to know if anyone knew where Dawn was, and that they suspected the Reeses were hiding her in their house. She added that they came inside and looked around a couple of times. The police, Pam went on, were also there, but Paul Sr., she said, was not. He had gone off somewhere with Timothy Keller.

"Later on, after everyone but the family had left," Pam said, "Barbara told me that Dawn's family thought Paul Sr. had kidnapped Dawn."

She added that at around 11:30 P.M. she went to bed, but about an hour later, a noise in the basement woke her up. She said she asked who was there, and Barbara answered, saying that she was just doing some laundry. However, Pam added, she didn't hear the washer or dryer start up. She told Detective Minor that she also heard Paul Sr.'s voice in the basement. Along with this, Pam discovered that Paul Jr. wasn't asleep in bed with her. However, she didn't give the incident much importance and went back to sleep.

Pam then told Minor that she got up the next morning and left with her father at around 7:00 A.M., and when she returned at around 1:30 P.M., the police were there again checking the house.

With no more questions to ask at the moment, Detective Minor thanked her and concluded the interview.

After interviewing Pam Winningham, Detective Minor next questioned fourteen-year-old Brian Reese, but the boy couldn't really give much information. Brian said that he knew Dawn and thought she was a nice girl.

"The last time I talked to her was on Saturday at our house," Brian told Minor. "She was playing cards with Jenny and Cindy."

He told Minor that he'd been asleep for most of the morning on Sunday, March 16, 1986, and hadn't even known that Dawn was there. After getting up, he said, he left and spent the day at some friends' house. He added that no one had talked about Dawn that night until the police and Dawn's relatives showed up.

Detective Minor thanked him and concluded the interview.

The next person Detective Roy West brought into the

Homicide Office for an interview was seventeen-year-old Timothy Keller, who confirmed that he had been in and out of the Reese house on the day Dawn Stuard had disappeared. Timothy said that he had come to the house on the morning of March 16, 1986, to pick up Paul Reese Jr. The two of them were going to take some items to a flea market on the west side of Indianapolis and try to sell them.

"The story was that early on Sunday morning, at around 9:30, Timothy Keller went over to the Reese house," recalled West. "He and Paul Reese Jr. were supposed to go to a flea market that morning to sell items they had stolen from their neighbors' yards."

When he arrived at the Reese house, Timothy told West, Paul Reese Sr. was the only one up and awake. However, within fifteen minutes of his arrival, Dawn showed up at the back door, and Timothy said he let her in before going down to the basement and waking up Paul Reese Jr. and his girlfriend, Pam Winningham. Timothy's story was the same one that others had told—leaving to pick up the items for the flea market, returning to find Pam's father, Cotton, out front, hearing about the altercation between Pam and her dad, then he and Paul Jr. jumping in his car and trying to make sure that Pam was okay. They followed Cotton's car for a short distance, but when they saw that Pam was apparently all right, they returned to the Reese house at about noon. Timothy added that when they returned to the house he saw Dawn and Paul Sr. coming up from the basement holding pool cues, then he and Paul Jr. left to go sell the items at the flea market.

West was unable to place Dawn anywhere outside of the Reese house that day, or find anyone who had seen her after this. He realized that the last person to have been seen with Dawn Marie Stuard was Paul Reese Sr.

After the interviews that night, it didn't take very much checking up on the Reeses for Detective Roy West to discover that the entire family had a reputation at the police department for both crime and trouble. West uncovered not only Paul Reese Sr.'s criminal record (he'd served time for various crimes, including trying to kill his girlfriend) but Barbara Reese's embezzlement conviction, and the arrest of the other two Reese sons, Jeremy and John, who were being held at the time of Dawn's disappearance at the Indianapolis Juvenile Correctional Center.

The neighbors in the 1400 block of North Bosart Street confirmed the Reese family's bad reputation. For years, the neighbors had been frightened and anxious because of the Reeses. Several of the neighbors told the news media that they felt like prisoners in their own homes. "People we talked to said they lived in fear and felt captive by this family," Indianapolis Metropolitan Police Department sergeant Dennis Fishburn told the local news media a number of years after Dawn's death. "People couldn't be themselves, they were so scared."

"I've never encountered a group of people in my life that scared me more," Mike Archer, a neighbor of the Reeses, told a reporter for the *Indianapolis Star* in 2008.

O n Tuesday, March 18, 1986, the day after the discovery of Dawn's body, the coroner's office performed an autopsy. While the crime scene search is often the greatest source of physical evidence in any homicide investigation, the next best source is usually the autopsy. Much like homicide detectives, many coroners also feel that they speak for the deceased. They realize that the autopsy is the last chance for the evidence that the victim's body holds to be discovered and used in the search for the killer, as well as in his or her eventual prosecution.

"As coroners, we are the last advocate to speak for the dead," Marion County (Indiana) chief deputy coroner Frances Kelly said. "The details and evidence that are on the body are the deceased's way of speaking to us."

Standard procedure was for one of the homicide detectives assigned to a murder case, usually the lead detective, to attend the autopsy, and Detective West attended Dawn's. Not only was it important for the detective to personally see what the coroner determined to be the cause and manner of death, which can tell a detective what other evidence needs to be searched for, but a homicide detective must be present at an autopsy in order to take custody of any evidence removed from the body that could prove crucial to the investigation.

At Dawn Marie Stuard's autopsy, the coroner, Dr. David W. Gauger, officially ruled her death a homicide. He determined that the cause of death had been asphyxiation caused by a thin, smooth object being violently pressed and held against her throat. The object had been bigger than a wire or rope, about a half inch or more wide. Dawn had also suffered blunt force trauma to the head, face, and neck, including a significant blunt force injury to the back of her head, which Dr. Gauger said was consistent with her head violently striking a flat, hard surface. This injury, he added, resulted in bleeding on the brain and had probably rendered her unconscious. In addition, he found tape residue on the girl's mouth and wrists, showing that she had been restrained and gagged. Dr. Gauger also found signs that Dawn had been sexually assaulted. He discovered forced sexual injuries to her vagina and anus. However, he did not find semen in the rectum or vaginal cavity. He also confirmed that there appeared to be carpet fibers on Dawn's hair and clothing. Finally, he said, fingernail marks on Dawn's neck and chin showed that she had struggled as she was strangled. The fingernail marks were her own, and had resulted from her trying to push away whatever was used to strangle her.

The autopsy findings sent Detective West back to the crime scene on Tuesday, March 18, to look for more evidence, especially anything related to the carpet fibers found in Dawn's hair and clothing. "I returned to the scene where we found her body and found similar carpet fibers up on the roadway near where the body was located, and off to the side of the road that led down into the ravine to where she had been dumped. Naturally, I called for crime lab technician Edwin Andresen, and collected these as evidence."

Since the Reese house was the last location where Dawn had been seen alive, West obtained a search warrant on March 22, 1986, for the Reese home. This was a little less than a week since he had examined the body at the crime scene, but he had needed this time to have evidence analyzed and to prepare the search warrant for a judge's signature. Knowing the Reese family's long history of crime and trouble, and after speaking with Timothy Keller and other witnesses, West had become more and more convinced that whatever had happened to Dawn Stuard, it had likely occurred in the Reese house.

Homicide detectives know that with a dumped body, if they can find the actual scene of the murder they will likely find evidence there. According to an article in the August 2004 issue of *Popular Science,* esteemed early-twentieth-century criminologist Edmond Locard stated in his exchange principle, "Whenever two objects come in contact, there is always a transfer of material." This means that in any violent struggle, evidence of it will often remain somewhere at the crime scene. In the 1953 book *Crime Investigation: Physical Evidence and the Police Laboratory,* the author Paul L. Kirk states, "Wherever [the killer] steps, whatever he touches, whatever he leaves, even unconsciously, will serve as silent evidence against him. Not only his fingerprints or his footprints, but his hair, the fibers from his clothes, the glass he breaks, the tool marks he leaves, the paint he scratches, the blood or semen he deposits or collects . . . all of these and more bear mute witness against him . . . Physical evidence cannot be wrong; it cannot perjure itself, it cannot be wholly absent . . . Only human failure to find it, study and understand it, can diminish its value."

Many murderers will leave a considerable amount of evidence behind, because murders often occur in the heat of the moment, and various scenarios may occur: the victim doesn't cooperate as anticipated; a gunshot or knife wound doesn't kill instantly; a victim fights back vigorously; an unexpected person suddenly shows up, etcetera. Therefore a killer may panic and drop important evidence; touch items and leave fingerprints behind; spatter blood where the killer can't see it in order to clean it up; and otherwise overlook and leave behind valuable evidence. West hoped that this fact would work to his advantage.

Because Dawn had not only suffered blunt force trauma, but had also been bound and gagged, West was certain that there had to be some evidence of the struggle Dawn had put up before she had been killed. He just had to search for it and find it.

Of all the evidence a homicide detective can recover in a murder investigation, one of the most important, of course, is the murder weapon. The coroner had said that Dawn had died from asphyxiation caused by a thin, smooth object being violently pressed against her throat. The pool cues in the basement of the Reese home seemed to Detective West to be a good match for this description. But West didn't overlook anything as possible evidence.

"With the search warrant at the Reese house," West said, "I had crime lab technician Edwin Andresen collect carpet samples that were similar to the fibers that were found at the scene where Dawn had been left. I also had newspapers and spray paint collected that were similar to the spray paint found on pieces of newspaper at the crime scene on East 23rd Street." In addition, he took a roll of duct tape.

Timothy Keller had told West that he had last seen Dawn and Paul Reese Sr. come up from the basement carrying pool cues. West had a strong feeling, based on what he had learned from and about the Reese family and from talking to various witnesses, that the murder of Dawn Marie Stuard had very likely occurred right there in the basement, so he gave it a thorough second, and third, search. It wasn't an easy task, because the basement was filled wall to wall with stacks of junk that West had to wade through in order to conduct his search. In a drawer in the basement he found a scrapbook that contained newspaper clippings about Dawn's murder. While this was not direct evidence, Detective West knew it could perhaps be useful later at the trial as supporting evidence. Following this, he continued his meticulous search. West's thoroughness eventually paid off, when he found a spot of blood on a brick furnace flue. But in 1986, that was far from conclusive.

While today crime lab technicians can test blood and bodily fluids for DNA that will pinpoint them as belonging to a specific person, that was not the case in 1986. Back then, all the crime lab could do was blood-typing, and the best that could do was eliminate certain individuals as the owner of the blood or bodily fluids. It couldn't say with certainty that the fluid came from a particular person.

"While in the basement, Andresen also collected what would eventually be referred to as item #63, a red sample, which turned out to be human blood," said West. "Unfortunately, in 1986 the most the crime lab could do was blood-typing, and it was found that it was type O blood, which was consistent with Dawn's blood type. It was a shame we didn't have DNA back then."

Therefore, while matching the blood drop to Dawn's blood type helped convince West that he was going in the right direction with his investigation, 38 percent of the world's population has type O blood, so, while helpful, this was just very circumstantial evidence. And unfortunately, the test used up all but a very tiny portion of the blood sample. West realized that in order to bring the investigation to a successful conclusion he was going to have to dig deeper and find more conclusive evidence. During his search of the Reeses' house, West found green and gold carpet fibers similar to the ones found on Dawn's body, not only in a waste can in the basement, but also on the ground outside the back of the house, and in their garage. West also had a brown station wagon owned by the Reeses towed to a secure lot for processing. Officer Andresen would later say that, while every other area of the car had been filled with junk, the rear of the station wagon had been cleared out, as if something had been transported back there. West had also learned that Paul

Reese Jr. had borrowed Timothy Keller's white Ford Pinto the night of Dawn's murder. It had been towed in later that night as part of another investigation, but a search of it didn't turn up anything of value to West's investigation.

West, however, didn't stop his search with just the Reese house and car. He knew that he still had some other sites to search, too. Paul Sr. had driven around with Timothy Keller for several hours late in the day that Dawn disappeared. West figured that Paul Sr. had probably had Timothy drive him around to scout out some places for use later as potential body dump locations.

"From talking with Timothy Keller, I learned that he had driven Paul Reese Sr. to several places on that Sunday evening, believed to have been after the murder was committed," West said. "He told me all of the locations they had gone to, and since I figured it could undoubtedly be very important to the case, I visited all of these places."

Around 8:00 P.M. on Sunday night, Keller said, Paul Sr. had called him and said he needed a ride to look at some tires that he would try to buy or possibly steal. One of the roads Paul Sr. had Keller drive along was the same one where Dawn was eventually found. They also drove to a few other locations, though Keller didn't know why.

West couldn't at the moment see any reason for Timothy to lie, and Paul Sr. had already told West that he had driven around with Timothy Keller the night Dawn disappeared. West also thought it likely that Timothy was suspicious of what Paul Sr. was doing, but that he was probably too frightened of Paul Sr., who was a scary man, to question his motives.

"One of the locations they drove to," West continued, "was East 19th Street and North Forest Manor Avenue, across from the Community Ball Park [less than a mile northwest of the Reese house and about a mile southwest of where Dawn's body had been found]. In that area I found a large [seventy-eight-by-thirty-eight-inch] section of green and gold carpet, some yellow nylon rope, a beer bottle, and a piece of the *Indianapolis Star* newspaper. This was significant in my mind because the carpet appeared similar to the carpet fibers found on Dawn's body, the carpet fibers found on the roadway on East 23rd Street, and the carpet fibers found in the basement of the Reese house. I would later learn, after having the carpet examined by the crime lab, that there was blood on this section of the carpet and that it was type O blood, which was consistent with Dawn's blood type."

However, as with the blood found in the basement of the Reese house, little could be done with this information at the time, and although West was hopeful, an examination of the beer bottle didn't turn up any usable fingerprints.

West continued the investigation, talking to everyone he could find who might know anything about the case and revisiting important sites several times to be certain nothing had been overlooked. He talked to several witnesses who said that Paul Reese Sr., usually a very calm and unflappable person, had seemed extremely nervous right after Dawn's disappearance. One neighbor, Archie

Ward, said that when Paul Sr. came to his house the night of Dawn's disappearance to ask for a ride and then eventually borrow a bicycle, he told him and his brother Jay that he needed to get out of the area because someone who thought he had kidnapped Dawn was chasing him. Jay Ward said that on the day after Dawn's death, Paul Reese Sr. had asked him to go down and check to see if the police were at the house on North Bosart Street, so he'd know whether it was safe to go back or not.

West questioned Paul Reese Sr. for a second time on April 15, 1986, but Paul Sr. stuck to the same story he had told originally and continued to deny having anything to do with Dawn's death.

The crime lab informed West that the carpet fibers found on Dawn Marie Stuard were similar to those West had recovered at the Reese house, and that the spray paint he had also recovered at the Reese house was similar to the paint found on the pieces of newspaper near Dawn's body. However, all they could say with certainty at the time was that they could be "of common origin." That was the best that forensic science could do in 1986; they could not be more definite. They could not say, without a doubt, that they were identical.

"All the crime lab could tell me was that the carpet fibers were consistent, that they had consistent characteristics with the carpet that was found at the Reese house," West said. "Blood type O was the same type as Dawn's blood, but not enough to establish that it was Dawn's blood. The crime lab also told me that the paint that was found on the newspaper at the crime scene was consistent with the spray paint found in the basement of the Reese house. Unfortunately, all of this was circumstantial."

Detective Sergeant Roy West worked tirelessly, searched over and over for more evidence, and interviewed dozens of possible witnesses. On September 15, 1986, West even spoke with James L. Reese, Paul Reese Sr.'s older brother. James claimed that his brother had admitted to him several days earlier that he'd had sex with Dawn and had killed her. While valuable, James's statement was still just hearsay and not direct evidence.

"We knew at the time that, with the dumping of the body, probably more than one person had to be involved," West said. "We had hoped that one of them would roll over on the other. We also couldn't exclude Timothy Keller from suspicion in the investigation. But eventually he took a polygraph test and passed it, and so, based on that, the prosecutor filed charges against Paul Reese Sr. and Paul Reese Jr."

On September 25, 1986, West arrested Paul Reese Sr. and Paul Reese Jr. and charged them with the murder of Dawn Marie Stuard. He also charged them with rape, criminal confinement, and criminal deviate conduct (a sexual assault other than a vaginal rape). Despite most of the evidence being circumstantial, West believed that, faced with a murder charge, Paul Reese Jr. might be willing to inform on his father in order to have his own charges dropped or reduced. But to West's disappointment, Paul Jr. stood fast.

In Indiana, once individuals have been arrested for

murder, they are almost always held in jail without bond until the trial. Because of this, witnesses and others with important information will many times come forward, since they no longer have to fear the person arrested. Also, many times those arrested will be willing to talk about making a deal with the prosecutor or be willing to inform on others involved in the case. West hoped that would prove true in the Dawn Marie Stuard case, but unfortunately, that didn't happen.

By January 1987, ten months after Dawn Marie Stuard's murder, the case had still not developed any more significant evidence or testimony. All West had was a lot of very circumstantial evidence. It deeply troubled him that he couldn't take the investigation any further, but he knew that if they went to trial with just the scant evidence they had, there was a very good chance that the father and son would be found not guilty, and that would be that. Because of double jeopardy, there could not be another trial down the road. And so, after conferring with the Prosecutor's Office, it was decided that the best course of action would be to drop the charges against Paul Reese Sr. and Paul Reese Jr.

Even though West knew that the charges could always be refiled in the future if more evidence in the case was ever to surface, he took little consolation in that fact.

"I felt terribly disappointed when we had to drop the charges," West said. "I had put a lot of time and work into this case, but more importantly this case involved a totally innocent young person who was sexually assaulted and brutally murdered. Her only crime had been trusting the Reese family."

Also disappointed in the decision was Dawn's father, Ted Stuard. From the moment he'd identified his daughter's body until the arrest of the Reeses in September 1986, Ted had tried to follow the case as closely as the police would allow him, waiting anxiously for the detectives to do something. He'd felt elated when the Indianapolis Police Department charged Paul Reese Sr. and Paul Reese Jr. with Dawn's murder, but devastated when they dropped the charges. Following that decision, Ted Stuard decided to move to Dayton, Ohio, after all. He couldn't believe that the police were releasing killers back onto the street. It was just too much. He had to get away. Indianapolis simply had too many bad memories.

Later that year, in November 1987, one of the Reeses' nearby neighbors, Mrs. Carol Luken, told a friend of hers who happened to be a deputy sheriff about some important information she had about the case. Carol was apparently deeply afraid of the Reeses, and of what they might do to her if they found out she'd spoken to the police, so it took over a year and a half before her conscience finally got the better of the fear. The deputy sheriff contacted Detective Roy West, who then spoke with Carol Luken himself. She told West that between 1:00 and 1:30 A.M. the day after Dawn Marie Stuard's disappearance, she had been up taking care of some newborn puppies and heard loud banging noises and voices coming from the Reese house nearby. She looked out her kitchen window and saw Paul Reese Jr. and another boy she didn't recognize pushing a car out of their backyard and into the street. The two then drove a different car, a station wagon, up to the back door of their house. Carol then said she witnessed Paul Reese Sr. and Paul Reese Jr. carry out of the house a six-to-seven-foot-long piece of rolled-up carpeting that sagged in the middle. Carol said she also saw the mother, Barbara Reese, open the tailgate of the station wagon and help her ex-husband and son load the piece of carpeting into the back of the station wagon. Then, with Barbara driving, she and Paul Sr. left in the station wagon with the headlights out. Paul Jr. followed them in a small white car. She wasn't sure what happened with the other youth.

"Unfortunately, this information wasn't known until well over a year after the case," West said. "But it was consistent with what witnesses who lived near the area where Dawn had been dumped told me. They said that at about 1:30 in the morning they heard their dogs start barking, extremely loud and for a long period of time. One of the witnesses saw the dogs looking over in the direction of where Dawn's body was eventually found, but it was extremely dark and the witness didn't see any lights. The witness figured the dogs were barking at some wild animal." West also added, "It is my belief that this area was chosen because Barbara Reese would normally have driven past this area to deliver the *Indianapolis Star* newspaper, and for her car to have been stopped in that area at that time of the morning wouldn't have drawn suspicion if seen by the neighbors."

However, even with this new piece of eyewitness testimony, the Prosecutor's Office still didn't think they had enough evidence to refile the charges. No one had seen a body, just a rolled-up carpet.

West returned disappointed from the Prosecutor's Office. "We were still waiting for someone to come forward who had direct knowledge about the crime before we could do anything further with the evidence we had collected," he said.

Detective West vowed, however, to never forget this case, his first unsolved homicide. He promised to always be on the lookout for any new evidence. As forensic science advanced over the following years, West would occasionally pull out the case file and see if there was anything more he could do with it. "In the 1990s, I had the Prosecutor's Office look again at the case," West said. "I also reinterviewed many people. But just nothing of significance developed that could bring this case forward."

Still, West refused to give up and renewed his vow to someday solve the case. "You never forget your unsolved cases," West said. "But if you have one with a child victim, it really stays with you. She was truly an innocent victim. She should have gone to her aunt's house rather than trust the Reeses."

FOUR

"Unfortunately, after we dropped the case, Paul Reese Sr. continued with his life of crime," Detective Roy West said—and not only that, he noted, but "with teaching his kids his way of life."

Indeed he did: "Lawless Legacy: Eastside Family Has 50 Convictions," read the headline of an article about the Reese family in the September 22, 2008, issue of the *Indianapolis Star* newspaper. And in the years since that article appeared, the family has continued to pile up more and more criminal convictions.

Left unprosecuted for Dawn Marie Stuard's murder, Paul Reese Sr. continued to lengthen his criminal record. Following his release after the State of Indiana dropped the charges in the murder case, Paul Reese Sr. went on to amass felony convictions and prison sentences for burglary (four times), robbery (twice), and drug possession.

Paul Sr.'s criminal record extended back to the 1960s, initially for relatively minor crimes. In January 1964 a court had convicted him of malicious trespass of a residence and fined him $1 and costs. Then in November 1971, a court again convicted him, this time of theft, and sentenced him to sixty days in jail. Paul Sr.'s criminal record suddenly turned deadly serious in 1979, however, when he pleaded guilty for attempted voluntary manslaughter. He admitted to the court that he had beat his forty-five-year-old girlfriend Helen K. Smith with a claw hammer. Paul Sr. actually called the Indianapolis Police Department himself soon after the attack and told them that he had tried to kill his girlfriend with the hammer. After making the call, Paul Sr. then briefly fled to Florida, but the police arrested him when he returned to Indiana soon afterward. They served a warrant on him while he was in the hospital recovering from an overdose of antidepressant medication. The police found Paul Sr.'s fingerprints at the crime scene, and the victim later identified him as her attacker. Paul Sr. claimed the attack had occurred during a blackout. He received a six-year prison sentence, though the State released him on parole on October 15, 1982. And though he spent four months in jail after being arrested for Dawn Marie Stuard's murder, after Paul Sr. was released from custody, he didn't remain free for long. In November 1989, a judge sentenced him to prison to serve a ten-year sentence for burglary. In this case, the court found him guilty of a Class B felony, meaning the crime was more serious than a normal burglary because it had special circumstances, such as his having been armed during the crime, or that the building he burglarized was a church. The State paroled him after less than six years, on July 19, 1995. His return to free society was short, however—four months later, in November 1995, a court sent him back to prison once again to serve two more years on another, different burglary charge. In that case, the court had found Paul Sr. guilty of a Class C felony for breaking into a home and trying to steal a VCR, though he was interrupted in the act by the residents returning home. He received parole on Christmas Day 1996 but soon had his parole revoked and was returned to prison.

Paul Reese Sr. never seemed to learn his lesson, though, not even after several years in prison. In May 1998, shortly after his release on the last burglary charge, a court again sentenced him for two counts of Class B felony robbery, one count resulting in a six-year sentence and the other in a sixteen-year sentence. In Indiana, robbery is defined as knowingly or intentionally taking the property of another by threatening to use force or by putting the person in fear. It is usually a Class C felony. It can, however, be upgraded to a Class B felony, as it was with Paul Sr., if the perpetrator is armed with a deadly weapon or the crime results in bodily injury to anyone other than the robber. The following year, in March 1999, a court convicted Paul Sr. of yet another Class C burglary and added an additional six years to his sentence. In December 2001, while still in prison serving his sentence for the last burglary charge, he received another year and six months in prison on charges of possession of marijuana, hash oil, or hashish. This is usually a Class A misdemeanor, but the court convicted Paul Sr. of the more severe Class D felony, which meant he had a larger than normal amount of the drug on him when arrested.

In addition to all of the above, the police had also arrested Paul Reese Sr. a number of times over the years for burglary, assault and battery, and even possession of a sawed-off shotgun, but those charges had been dropped for various reasons.

The matriarch of the family, Barbara Reese, like her ex-husband, didn't set much of an example for her six children. According to the article in the *Indianapolis Star*, she had been arrested in the 1970s on federal embezzlement charges for stealing money from the bank where she worked. She pleaded guilty and a court sentenced her to eighteen months of probation.

Paul Reese Sr.'s older brother, James L. Reese, the same one who told Detective Roy West in 1986 that Paul Sr. had confessed raping and killing Dawn Marie Stuard to him, also shared in the family's propensity for crime. The police in Arizona arrested him for child molestation and dangerous crimes against children. He began serving a twenty-year sentence for the crimes in December 1997 and is presently at the Arizona State Prison Complex in Tucson.

Of Paul and Barbara Reese's six children, so far only the two girls, Jenny and Cynthia, have managed to stay out of jail. The four boys—Paul Jr., born in December 1969; John, born in January 1971; Brian, born in February 1972; and Jeremy, born in March 1973—all have criminal records, both individually and as a group; according to the article in the *Indianapolis Star*, in 1989 the police arrested all four of the Reese boys for the attempted burglary of an eighty-five-year-old woman's house. From then on, the boys continued to rack up the criminal convictions.

Paul Reese Jr., the oldest son, received a two-year prison term in September 1990 for the attempted burglary. He was charged with conspiracy to commit burglary, which means that a person has agreed to and taken concrete steps to take part in a crime with others. In July 1994, he followed that up with a six-year prison sentence for a Class C felony, reckless homicide, which in Indiana involves killing someone by acting in a reckless manner but without premeditation. This can be anything from the reckless operation of a motor vehicle to shooting a gun into a crowd. And then in December 1994, a court again convicted him of conspiracy to commit burglary and sentenced him to another two years in prison.

Despite a period of avoiding serious trouble after that, Paul Jr. once more ran afoul of the law when in April 2003 a judge sentenced him to a year imprisonment for operating a motor vehicle while intoxicated and resisting law enforcement. A few years later, in June 2008, Paul Jr. received another two-year sentence for resisting law enforcement, along with a six-month sentence for mischief, defined as the damaging or destroying of another person's property. Though usually a misdemeanor, it can rise to the level of a felony, as it did with Paul Jr., if the property loss is extensive. In November 2009, he garnered himself another six-month sentence for mischief, and then in March 2011 he received a one-year prison sentence for possession of drug paraphernalia. This last violation involves possessing some device or raw material for use in the consumption of illegal drugs.

The next oldest son, John, has the shortest record of the four Reese boys. In addition to his juvenile record, a judge in February 1990 sentenced him to ten years in prison on two counts of burglary, stemming from the attempted burglary he committed with his brothers.

The youngest Reese son, Jeremy, also spent time in juvenile detention, and like the other members of his family, has had a number of brushes with the law as an adult. In March 1995, a court sentenced him to three years in prison for Class C felony burglary, and then two weeks after that he had six months added to his sentence for failure to return to lawful detention/escape following his failure to report to a detention facility after being granted a special leave. Following these convictions, in August 1995, he received a sentence of three and a half years in prison for theft/receiving stolen property.

Starting in 1998, Jeremy began amassing a number of jail and prison sentences for very serious driving offenses. In February 1998, he received an eight-month jail sentence for operating a motor vehicle while being a habitual traffic violator; in July 2000 he garnered himself a two-year prison sentence for operating a vehicle after a lifetime suspension; and then in December 2001 he received another two-year sentence for the same offense. In Indiana, if a person commits enough very serious driving offenses, a court can suspend the person's driving privileges for life, after which it becomes a felony if the person is caught driving. In February 2004, a court convicted him once more of operating a motor vehicle after a lifetime suspension, but also convicted him of resisting law enforcement and possession of marijuana, hash oil, or hashish during this same incident. The court sentenced him to a total of four years in prison for these offenses. Following this, in November 2005, a court convicted Jeremy of the same three charges as it did in February 2004, and then in June 2008, a court once more convicted him of operating a motor vehicle after a lifetime suspension. In October 2008, Jeremy received a sentence of one and a half years in prison for attempted theft/receiving stolen property, after which a judge added six months to his sentence for failure to return to lawful detention/escape. Finally, in January 2011, shortly after his release from prison, a court once more convicted him of operating a motor vehicle after a lifetime suspension, along with two counts of resisting law enforcement. Jeremy received a total of eight years in prison for this incident.

Notably in Jeremy's case, as in the case of several other members of the Reese family, they seemed to be out committing crimes when they should've been serving prison sentences. Sometimes they were actually already in prison when charged with other crimes that occurred before the incarceration, but the more common situation was that they simply weren't serving the full sentence imposed. Indiana, like most states, has a "good time" rule, which gives prisoners a day off of their sentence for every day of good behavior. Also, prisoners can have time taken off of their sentence by obtaining various educational diplomas while in prison. Along with this, practically every state suffers from prison overcrowding, and many are under court order to reduce their population. Consequently, many prisoners get an early release simply to make way for new prisoners. And finally, often individuals will be out on bond, rather than in prison, while appealing a sentence.

Brian Reese, the second-youngest son, also had a lengthy juvenile record—reportedly four true findings (found guilty) for conversion (theft) in 1985, conversion again in 1987, burglary in 1988, and conspiracy to commit theft in 1989.

As an adult Brian has had a number of misdemeanor arrests, starting with resisting law enforcement, disorderly conduct, driving while suspended, and having no insurance in September 1992, for which the judge sentenced him to a diversion program. In November 1993, the police again arrested Brian for driving while suspended, and the judge again put him into a diversion program. In February 2007, the police once more arrested Brian for driving while suspended, and this time he received a fine and jail time. The police also arrested Brian for check deception in 1995, but the charges were dropped.

Along with misdemeanors, the police also arrested Brian for several felonies. In February 1991 he received a three-year prison sentence for conspiracy (again involving the burglary of the eighty-five-year-old woman's home), and in December 1999 the police arrested him for felony resisting law enforcement. In this last case, Brian ran a sheriff's deputy off the road and then fled from the police. And yet, despite having near constant run-ins with the police throughout his life, Brian's real problems with the law began in 2008.

It started on May 29, 2008, with theft and forgery charges. In this case Brian reportedly entered a woman's house on East St. Joseph Street and took, among other things, money, credit cards, several pieces of expensive and unusual jewelry, and a pad of blank checks. The detectives investigating the case found several of the blank checks had been filled out and cashed. The name the checks had been made out to: Brian Reese. Also, a quick check of pawnshops turned up several pieces of the jewelry that had been taken during the crime. In Indiana, when a person pawns something, the pawn dealer must have positive identification of the person pawning the item and take a fingerprint. The person pawning the stolen jewelry: Brian Reese. The police swore out a forgery and theft warrant for Brian. However, this crime would turn out to be minor compared to what followed soon afterward.

FIVE

Although the Reese family certainly had its struggles when it came to obeying the law, unfortunately they weren't unique or even that unusual a crime family. Criminal conduct seems to run in families just like any other sociological trait.

The most famous family of criminals known to sociologists was the "Juke" family, a pseudonym used by the original researcher of this clan, Richard L. Dugdale. Dugdale was a nineteenth-century sociologist and a member of the executive committee of the Prison Association of New York, which, in 1874, had assigned him the task of checking out the various county jails within the state and then letting the association know about their conditions. The original intent of the study, therefore, was simply to inspect and report back on the status of the state's county jails.

However, as Dugdale began his inspection of the county jails, he became intrigued when he discovered that many of the inmates in the various penal facilities were related to one another either by blood or by marriage. He began an investigation into one such family and assigned them the code name Juke. Through his research, Dugdale managed to trace the Jukes back five generations, to 1792. He identified 709 individuals in his study, 504 blood relatives and the remainder related by marriage. Of these 709 individuals, Dugdale managed to verify that 140 of them had amassed an amazing number of criminal violations, including convictions for theft, assault, rape, and murder. He estimated that between 1800 and 1875, the state of New York spent approximately 1.3 million dollars in legal and administrative fees, incarceration costs, and other associated expenses because of the Juke family.

Dugdale eventually published his findings in a best-selling 1877 book titled *The Jukes: A Study in Crime, Pauperism, Disease, and Heredity.* Although in his book Dugdale blamed most of the Juke family's crime problems on the environment the family lived in (which he said then caused the children who grew up in these surroundings to pick up the criminal habits of the adults and pass them on to their own children), unfortunately supporters of eugenics seized on the study as proof of their argument that criminals carried bad genes.

Eugenics was a social movement popular in the first half of the twentieth century. Its adherents believed that many of the problems of society (which included, in their estimation, crime, feeblemindedness, and sexual deviancy, among others) could be traced back to bad genes, and that criminals could in addition be identified through certain physical features. Because of the growth of the eugenics movement, and the pressure it was able to put on politicians, the idea of forcibly sterilizing undesirable individuals took root in American society and lasted until the 1960s, and is today looked upon as a shameful part of American history. But still, while the Juke family became the rallying cry for the supporters of eugenics, they, like the Reeses, were hardly unique.

Another such family was the Bogles. The police first became aware of the Bogle family in 1961 when Dale Vincent Bogle, known as Rooster, moved from Texas to the Willamette Valley area of Oregon. Rooster had already served considerable time in prison, and soon after arriving in Oregon he began instructing his children in crime, teaching them how to break into stores and steal semitrailers.

"Rooster raised us to be outlaws," Tracey Bogle, Rooster's youngest child, told the *New York Times* on August 21, 2002. It was less nature than nurture; the children said that Rooster would berate them and call them cowards if they didn't do what he demanded. He would put intense pressure on his children to break the law. Around eighty members of the family (some related by blood, some related by marriage) have been sent to jail or prison, Tracey told KATU News in Salem, Oregon on January 10, 2010.

Then there were the Ramseys. The State of Missouri

executed Roy Ramsey on April 14, 1999, for the murder of an elderly couple during a robbery he had committed with his brother Billy at the couple's home. Reportedly, upon returning home with the loot they had taken in the robbery, the two brothers had split the haul with their mother. Nine of Roy's ten brothers served time in prison, four of them convicted of murder, and one even became the victim of a murder himself after being released from prison.

Where Dugdale originally blamed a bad environment for the generations of Juke family crime, and the supporters of eugenics blamed bad genes, a number of scientific studies have been conducted over the years to continue examining the question of what causes crime to run in some families but not in others.

The Institute of Criminology at Cambridge University in Great Britain conducted one of these studies, which was reported in 2009. This research involved 411 men that the researchers followed from age eight to age forty-eight. The researchers found that in this group, 48 percent of the men with fathers who had been convicted of a crime also eventually became convicted of a crime, compared to only 19 percent of the men with fathers who hadn't been convicted of a crime. Also having a significant effect on a study subject's likelihood of criminal activity, the study found, was having a sibling involved in crime.

Interestingly, the study also found that the fathers with a criminal conviction often married women with a criminal conviction. The researchers reasoned that this was likely because these types of individuals ran in the same social circles, and shared many of the same values, which would then attract them to each other. As might be imagined, the researchers found that this marriage of individuals with criminal convictions increased their children's likelihood of also being convicted of a crime.

The researchers also discovered that although a majority of the convicted mothers in the study were married to convicted fathers, even when the researchers cancelled out this factor, they found that having a mother who had been convicted of a crime significantly increased the probability that any male children would also be convicted of a crime. In the study, the researchers found that 54 percent of the men that had a mother who had been convicted of a crime also eventually became convicted of a crime, compared to only 23 percent of the men whose mother had not been convicted of a crime. And as might be imagined, having both parents convicted of a crime increased those chances even more. The researchers discovered that in three-fourths of the families with both a convicted father and mother, a male child would also eventually have a criminal conviction.

The Cambridge researchers concluded in their study, which, according to the September 5, 2012, issue of *The Independent,* was published in the *Journal of Legal and Criminal Psychology,* "A convicted family member influenced a boy's likelihood of delinquency independent of other important factors such as poor housing, overcrowding, and low school attainment."

But one of the most interesting findings of this study

was how crime appeared to cluster in certain families. The researchers found that only 6 percent of the families they studied accounted for half of all the criminal convictions in their research.

Other research projects have shown similar results. For example, a study in Sweden, conducted between 1973 and 2004, looked at 12.5 million individuals. The researchers obtained information on criminal convictions from the Swedish Crime Register and were able to establish family connections between the study subjects via the Swedish Total Population Register and census data, as well as other population registry information. The study found a strong correlation for crime to run in families; the closer the family members, the stronger the correlation. The strongest threat for crime running in families was in groups of close genetic relatives living together. The study, though finding significant correlations for crime between parents and children, and between siblings, interestingly enough, didn't find any correlation for criminal behavior between biologically unrelated adopted siblings living together.

In a similar, but much smaller, research project, the Pittsburgh Youth Study, researchers looked at 1,500 males starting at age seven and continuing up until they were thirty. The results showed that having a father, mother, brother, sister, uncle, aunt, grandfather, or grandmother convicted of a crime increased the chances of the study subjects also being convicted of a crime. The Pittsburgh Youth Study found that the father above all other relatives turned out to be the best predictor of a son's future involvement in crime. However, in an interesting finding of yet another similar study, researchers found that the arrest records of stepfathers and biological fathers were similarly correlated with a male child also being arrested and convicted of a crime, which seems to point to the importance of environment in promoting criminal behavior.

Young female family members can also be adversely affected, though in a lesser way. For example, a study published in May 2011 in *Trends & Issues in Crime and Criminal Justice* found that a daughter who had a father with a criminal record, but a mother with no criminal record, had a 26.7 percent chance of eventually having a criminal record herself, whereas for a son under the same circumstances the chances were 48.5 percent. For a daughter with both a father and a mother with a criminal record, the odds of the daughter having a criminal record rose to 43.8 percent, compared to 66.9 percent for a son.

According to an article in a 2009 issue of *Criminal Behavior and Mental Health,* titled "Association of Criminal Convictions between Family Members: Effects of Siblings, Fathers, and Mothers," social scientists studying criminal families have come up with five possible reasons for this clustering of statistics. The first reason is that criminal families may be trapped in environments that tend to raise the likelihood of crime (such as poverty, substandard housing, poor discipline practices with children, and having teenage parents with poor parenting skills). The second reason is that individuals with criminal records often tend to gravitate to each other, and consequently infuse their children with their own antisocial attitudes. The third reason is that children tend to imitate their parents and older siblings, and if these individuals are criminals, then it is likely that the children imitating them will be criminals also. The fourth reason has to do with labeling—for instance, whether the authorities are more likely to investigate and prosecute an individual from a known criminal family such as the Jukes, the Bogles, or the Reeses than an individual from a family not known to the authorities. Likewise, scientists also wonder whether the family members of a clan well known to the police see prosecution as almost inevitable, therefore reasoning that the police will eventually stop and arrest them for some reason, so they might as well just go ahead and commit the crime, thus bringing about a self-fulfilling prophecy. The final reason goes back to the days of eugenics and suggests that crime clusters in certain families because of genetic traits passed on from parent to child; that the children in certain families, because of their genes, simply have a greater disposition toward crime.

Researchers of inherited traits have found in a number of studies that certain psychological and emotional problems can definitely be passed on from parent to child through their genes. Some researchers have argued, however, that the environment the individuals with these psychological and emotional problems are raised in, rather than the genes themselves, will often decide whether or not these problems will result in a life of crime. Consequently, criminality itself may not be inherited, but the psychological and emotional problems (which with the wrong environment can lead to a life of crime) may be. However, occasionally there are also biological causes. In an article by H.G. Brunner, appearing in a 1993 issue of *Science*, researchers in a study of tendencies toward violence passed on from parent to child looked at a large Dutch family that had a long history of violent crime among the male members. The researchers found that the men in the family who exhibited violent tendencies had a defect in a gene that controlled an important neurochemical in their brain. The men lacking the neurochemical in their brain were prone to committing acts of rape and assault.

Of course, many researchers believe that it is more likely that a combination of environment and heredity is what causes the problem. Whatever the answer, the members of the Reese family continued to rack up one criminal conviction after another, year after year. Police officers involved in the many criminal investigations of the Reese family never saw much improvement or any signs of positive change within the family. And some police officers, such as Detective Sergeant Roy West, never forgot their involvement with the Reese family, or in his case, his vow to one day solve the Dawn Marie Stuard murder.

It would be more than a quarter of a century before he finally got his chance.

SIX

The onset of June in Indiana often brings with it hot, sultry weather that can last until the middle of September. The hot and sticky weather seems to shorten tempers and bring about an increase in violence. June 2008 was no exception—and it began a summer season of violence during which the murder rate increased greatly compared with the winter and spring months. By July 2008, the police in Indianapolis were responding to a murder every other day.

Naturally, this large number of murders garnered a considerable amount of news media coverage, which in turn put the police department under a lot of added pressure to do something about the violence. Not surprisingly, the murder rate is often seen as a measure of the crime level and safety of a community. The police department made a number of public promises to do all they could to stem the violence, but most of this was simply verbal self-defense. There was little that the police could really do to prevent these murders. Most murders occur on the spur of the moment and happen inside residences or in secluded areas, or they occur because a person has become so enraged that he or she loses control, and no amount of increased patrol will prevent any of those crimes. The best the police can do is to try to take a known dangerous person off the street. This won't necessarily stop more murders from occurring in the future, but it is all the police can do.

Homicide detectives in Indianapolis in June and early July 2008 found themselves working overtime, trying to investigate their previous cases while also handling the sudden rush of new cases. Every one of the homicides they investigated was in itself a tragic case, with victims whose lives had been cut short. But three of the murders committed in July 2008 were different: They appeared to be connected. The police quickly realized that the three had all apparently been committed by the same killer. The homicide detectives knew that they needed to apprehend this murderer quickly. If they didn't, this person would very likely kill again.

The first of the three murders believed committed by this serial murderer was that of Clifford Haddix, a sixty-nine-year-old United Auto Workers retiree with no police record, and who was by all reports a solid, upstanding citizen. On July 6, 2008, he died during an apparent robbery at his house in the 3000 block of East Newton Avenue. A neighbor, William Rinehart, was sitting on his porch and saw Haddix come home at 9:10 P.M. At 10:20 P.M. Rinehart saw that the lights were still on at Haddix's house. Rinehart knew that Haddix always went to bed before that time, so he walked over to check on him. He found the front door open and saw Haddix on the floor. Rinehart immediately called 911.

According to the police, it was later ascertained that at around 10:00 P.M. someone had kicked in the front door of Haddix's house and murdered him before ransacking his house and taking a number of valuable items, including firearms and jewelry. Witnesses later said that they had heard three shots, which unfortunately wasn't uncommon for that area. People living in bad neighborhoods usually seek cover when they hear gunshots; they don't go out to investigate them. The police officers answering the 911 call found Haddix lying on the hallway floor near his bedroom, with gunshot wounds to his head. The coroner officially pronounced him dead at 10:34 P.M. Homicide detective Randall Cook, the lead detective on the case, recovered three spent 9 mm casings and two spent bullets at the scene. The autopsy would show that Haddix had died from those three gunshots to the head. The neighbors who lived nearby were stunned upon hearing of Clifford Haddix's murder, as they all knew him to be a kind old man who had never done anything to deserve such a death.

"Sat on the porch and we talked every day, seven days a week," neighbor William Rinehart told the news media.

Within a week, the police would arrest Brian Reese for the burglary and murder of Clifford Haddix. They would also arrest Brian's father, Paul Reese Sr., and Brian's girlfriend, Lona Bishop, charging them as accessories to the crime.

According to homicide detective Randall Cook, Brian Reese and Clifford Haddix had never met before that night. Reportedly, Brian, when looking for a house to burglarize, would knock on the door and even on the windows of a likely target. If the residents answered, he would ask them about doing odd jobs, and if they didn't answer he would burglarize the house.

Haddix had apparently been targeted by Brian because he kept his house in such good shape. "He kept his house and yard in immaculate shape," Detective Cook said about the reason Brian likely targeted Mr. Haddix's house. "He was pretty well-to-do for that neighborhood, and his house showed it."

On the evening of July 6, 2008, according to Detective Cook, Haddix had gone to bed a half hour or so before Brian knocked at his door and on his windows. Haddix either didn't hear the knocking or chose to ignore it, and Brian, thinking that no one was home, forced open the front door. This got Haddix out of bed, and he confronted Brian in the hallway of his house. Brian shot Haddix multiple times, killing him. Brian then ransacked the house, taking firearms, jewelry, and other items.

An overheard conversation soon cracked the case. A local deputy sheriff who worked off duty as a security officer at an apartment complex spoke to a man who worked maintenance there, and who told the deputy sheriff that he had overheard a conversation between two people discussing a burglary where the victim had been killed. The maintenance worker didn't have any names, but it was enough to give the detectives a place to start, and after considerable investigation, it led them to Brian Reese's girlfriend, Lona Bishop, and through her to Brian Reese.

Lona Bishop eventually turned State's Witness and gave the police detailed information about the Haddix murder and other crimes. She told the police that on the night that Clifford Haddix was killed, she had been walking with Paul Reese Sr. on East Newton Avenue, headed toward the Big Lots store in the nearby Twin-Aire Shopping Center, when Paul Sr. received a text from his son Brian. After reading the text, Paul Sr. told Lona that there was a change of plans, and they were now going to go meet Brian. As they neared Haddix's home on East Newton Avenue, Lona said, she saw Brian knock on the front door and then walk around and knock on the windows on the east side of the house. When he received no answer, she said, he then walked up to the front door and forced it open with his shoulder. She added that all this time Paul Sr. was acting very suspicious, seeming nervous and jumpy. Lona told the police that soon after Brian entered the house she heard three gunshots. She insisted that she waited down the street during the Haddix burglary, but that Paul Reese Sr. acted as a lookout outside the house and kept in contact with Brian over a walkie-talkie. She and Paul Sr. met Brian a few minutes later. She said Brian was out of breath, panicked, and nervous. He also carried a black backpack. The two men, she claimed, then dropped her off at her house on Hamilton Avenue and left. However, when the police later served a search warrant on Lona's house, they recovered a United Auto Workers watch that had belonged to Clifford Haddix, some of his other property, and several items the officers believed had been taken in other burglaries.

O n July 8, two days after the Haddix murder, the police answered a call about gunshots at a house in the 200 block of North Hendricks Place. There, uniformed officers found the bodies of twenty-eight-year-old Crystal Joy Jenkins and twenty-two-year-old Demetrius Allen. Both had been shot to death. The officers called for Homicide.

Allen, the homicide detectives would learn, had made his living as a full-time crack cocaine dealer. Not as a high-level dealer, the police would later say, but rather one who made his money by keeping the crackheads in his neighborhood supplied. Jenkins was not another dealer but simply Allen's live-in girlfriend and a crack user.

The couple lived near Lona Bishop, in a run-down rented house with beat-up furniture, and kept their clothing in plastic bags. It wasn't a very high standard of living, due to Allen not making that much money as a drug dealer, particularly since he supplied his girlfriend with drugs for free, but also because the couple knew that they needed to be ready to leave with just a few moments' notice if they ever thought the police were onto them. And while Allen and Jenkins did everything they could not to come to the attention of the police, they always made certain that the local crackheads knew where to find them. This would be their undoing.

Through their investigation (and an eventual confession by Paul Reese Sr.), the homicide detectives learned that on the day Jenkins and Allen were murdered, Brian Reese, Paul Reese Sr., and Brian's girlfriend, Lona Bishop, had been smoking crack cocaine in Lona's house at 215 North Hamilton Avenue, on the east side of Indianapolis.

Both Brian and Paul Sr. would later talk to the authorities about their heavy drug use. Paul Sr. said that he started drinking at fourteen, first used marijuana at age twenty-three, and started using cocaine in 1994. Paul Sr. admitted that he used cocaine heavily, on a daily basis, and that he would inject it. He said he would use it every day if he could afford it, and that he had been on a three-week binge just before his arrest in 2008. He also used heroin and LSD. He added that he would have anger control problems while on drugs; that absolutely anything would set him off.

His son Brian also had a long history of substance abuse. According to a self-report in a court document, "He began using alcohol and marijuana at a young age. He reportedly consumes alcohol 'all the time,' and uses marijuana every now and then. He uses cocaine and methamphetamines 'all the time.' He said he was under the influence of cocaine at the time of the [most recent] incident."

On July 8, 2008, Lona and Paul Sr. had been smoking crack all day long; Brian, however, had been doing it for several days. Consequently, he was flying high from the drug when he suddenly realized that they were out of crack. They had smoked it all and needed more. But there was a problem. They didn't have any more money. They had already spent everything they had on the drugs they'd smoked that day.

"Don't worry," Brian told his father and girlfriend. "I know where to get some more." He picked up a .38 caliber revolver and put it in his pocket.

Brian and Paul Sr. then left Lona's house and walked a block west to the 200 block of North Hendricks Place, where Allen and Jenkins lived. Brian and Paul Sr. didn't go to the front door. If a person wanted to buy drugs he or she went to the side door, which opened into the kitchen. Brian knocked on the door, and when Allen saw who it was he opened it. He had sold drugs to Brian many times. Brian and Paul Sr. then forced their way into the house, and Brian shot Allen in the head and torso with the .38 caliber revolver, killing him.

"There was probably very limited conversation," said homicide detective Mike Mitchell, the lead investigator on the case. "We found Allen on the kitchen floor just beyond the door."

Jenkins, who had been in the house with Allen, screamed and ran into the family room. Brian and Paul Sr. chased after her and then shot her with a 25 mm. semiautomatic pistol. She fell to the floor, but wasn't dead, so they shot her four more times with the 25 mm.

semiautomatic. Paul Reese Sr. would later tell the police that they kept shooting her because she wouldn't shut up. She'd kept moaning and gurgling.

Which one of the two Reese men actually shot Crystal Joy Jenkins was a bit unclear—it was possible that only one of them had killed both her and Demetrius Allen, switching weapons in between shootings, but the more likely version of events was that both men were involved. It was undisputed that Brian had killed Allen, but the homicide detectives said that Paul Sr. wasn't very forthcoming about which of them actually shot Jenkins. Also, the police wanted to know, where had the 25 mm. semiautomatic pistol come from? Homicide detectives think it was likely that Paul Sr. had carried it with him to the house. He had already served time in prison for two other robberies. Paul Reese Sr., who made a deal with the police to cooperate in order to avoid multiple murder charges, would claim sometime after this that Brian had been the one who did all the shooting in the house on North Hendricks Place. While the police suspected that Paul Sr. may have done more than he said, they couldn't prove it because Brian wouldn't talk with Detective Mitchell. He stood on his right to remain silent.

Since Brian had bought crack cocaine at the house on Hendricks Place a number of times before, he knew that Allen kept his stash of drugs on top of the refrigerator. Brian helped himself to it. He may have taken other items as well, but the house existed in such a state of disarray from Allen and Jenkins's lifestyle that the police were unable to tell for certain whether Brian and Paul Sr. had taken anything besides the drugs.

Detective Mitchell, of course, searched the crime scene thoroughly for fingerprints, shell casings, and anything else left behind by the murderer that would point the police in the right direction. Also, during the service of the search warrant at Lona's house, the police, in addition to finding Clifford Haddix's property, also recovered a 25 mm. Titan semiautomatic pistol. The crime lab would later confirm that this was the gun used to kill Crystal Joy Jenkins.

But it wasn't the crime scene that would solve this case. It would be the autopsies. The next day, the coroner removed multiple bullets from the two victims, and the crime lab ran them through their computer system, which compared them to other known and unknown bullets.

"It was all forensics that solved this case," said Mitchell. "The crime lab got a hit on the .38 caliber bullet that killed Demetrius Allen."

When the crime lab technicians checked the bullet taken from Allen several days later, they found that it matched a bullet taken from another person that Brian Reese was known to have shot.

Interestingly enough, this wasn't the first time Detective Mitchell had encountered Brian Reese. "When I was a young officer on the east side," he said, "I chased Brian all the time for stealing bicycles and cars." It was clear, though, that Brian had graduated to more serious crimes since then. When Detective Randall Cook, the lead detective in the Haddix case, eventually questioned Brian Reese, he said he felt extremely uncomfortable. "Talking to Brian Reese was like talking to Lucifer," he said. "His eyes were real piercing and you could see the evil in them. He was one of those guys that when you talk to them the hair on the back of your neck stands up."

Eventually all of the investigation in both the Haddix and the Allen and Jenkins cases would lead homicide detectives to Brian Reese—but before they ever spoke to him, first the detectives had to work the leads they had. In Detective Cook's case, that meant Lona Bishop. Cook believed she might have been a witness to Haddix's murder, and he needed to get her to talk before he could go after Brian Reese. Cook decided to bring Lona in for questioning, and called on some district detectives to assist him—usually a very routine matter. But unfortunately, this request would instead lead to an incredible and tragic chain of events that was anything but routine.

SEVEN

On July 10, 2008, four narcotics detectives sat in their office in the basement of the Southeast District Headquarters on South Shelby Street in Indianapolis, Indiana. As the name implied, the district the detectives worked for covered the southeast portion of the city. The four-man unit mostly took care of smaller drug problems in the district. Catching the drug kingpins and making the huge drug busts usually fell to the main narcotics unit down at police headquarters, but the work the four men did contributed significantly to the quality of life for the residents of their district. The detectives, who worked the 11:00 A.M. to 7:00 P.M. shift, were just getting ready to start work when the telephone rang. One of the men walked over and picked it up, then spoke for several minutes while taking some notes on a pad.

"Okay, we'll take care of it," he said finally and then hung up the telephone. When he walked back over to the other three detectives, they all looked at him with raised eyebrows. "Detective Cook in Homicide wants us to give him a hand," he told them. "He wants us to go over and pick up a lady on Hamilton Avenue and take her down to the Homicide Office for an interview. I guess they're busier than hell because they've had a real slew of murders lately. Anyway, she lives at . . ."—he looked down at the notes he had taken—". . . uh, 215 North Hamilton."

The 200 block of North Hamilton Avenue sat in a poor working-class neighborhood on the east side of Indianapolis. The narcotics detectives knew that part of their district well. They had been in the area, a neighborhood infested with crackheads, many times.

"Which murder does he want to talk to her about?" one of the other detectives asked.

"I don't know. He didn't say. But she couldn't be too important or else he would've come out and got her himself. He did tell me though not to make a big show of it, but to try and keep it low key." He again looked down at the notes he had taken. "According to him, the woman's name is Lona Bishop. Apparently she doesn't have any kind of record or anything, so this should be pretty easy."

The four detectives—Ryan Vanoeveren, Chad Osborne, Chris Smith, and Aaron Tevebaugh—had all done jobs like this before. All of the various detective units on the Indianapolis Metropolitan Police Department routinely tried to help one another out when they could. Besides, this one seemed like an easy enough task—it shouldn't take that long, and since, according to Detective Cook, Lona apparently wasn't dangerous, the four decided that there wouldn't be any reason to conduct any surveillance first. They'd just whip by and get her, and then go about their real business.

The four detectives decided that Smith and Vanoeveren would go up to Lona's front door, and Osborne and Tevebaugh would cover the rear of the house. Not that they really expected her to try to run; if she'd been a flight risk, they figured Homicide would have come out to get her themselves. Doing it that way was just standard procedure. No one felt overly concerned about the task.

The detectives talked for a few minutes about the other business they had planned to take care of that day, and then gathered up their paperwork and equipment and headed for the exit, wanting to get this errand for Homicide out of the way so they could move on to serious business. The Southeast District of Indianapolis covered a large area, and the narcotics detectives assigned there had all of the work they could handle.

Once out in the parking lot, the officers found the weather hot and muggy, pretty typical for Indiana in July. It was just after 2:00 P.M., and the detectives knew it was probably going to get hotter before evening finally arrived. Because their Chevrolet TrailBlazer had been parked in the sun, they cranked up the air-conditioning before pulling the vehicle out of the parking lot and heading north on Shelby Street. Lona Bishop's house on Hamilton Avenue sat less than three miles away.

A few minutes later, Osborne and Tevebaugh dropped

off Smith and Vanoeveren at a corner near Lona Bishop's house and then headed to the alley that ran up behind 215 North Hamilton Avenue. They idled toward the alley in order to allow the two other detectives time to reach the small, one-story, wood-frame house with a brick porch.

Turning into the narrow alley, Osborne and Tevebaugh cruised slowly down the potholed asphalt that ran behind Hamilton Avenue, skirting a pile of old lumber and used tires someone had dumped in the alley. Meanwhile, Smith and Vanoeveren strolled casually down the sidewalk; though in civilian clothing, they wore their Glock semiautomatic pistols in holsters on their sides and their badges on chains around their necks. Since they worked narcotics, they didn't wear uniforms, but rather dressed in clothing that would blend in the neighborhoods they worked. If they didn't want to be spotted as the police, they took off the Glocks and badges. In this case, though, it didn't matter if the people in the neighborhood knew they were the police. When the two men reached 215, they turned and started up the broken concrete walk. There was no thought of extra caution beyond what a police officer normally employs, or of any extra danger beyond what a police officer normally faces. This was just a routine task.

A few moments later, just before they reached the door, a man who looked to be in his mid-thirties, with sandy hair and several days' growth of beard, opened the door and started out. He stopped instantly when he saw the two officers. Smith and Vanoeveren identified them-

selves and asked if Lona Bishop was there. The detectives
would later say that they had no idea at the time who this
man was, but he apparently thought they did. The man
looked both surprised and alarmed, and then stammered
something about having to put his dog up before he
could let the officers in. He then hurried back in the
house and slammed the door shut. The officers heard
him lock it. They soon also heard the sound of running
and commotion inside the house, and the sound of the
man shouting, "It's the Feds! It's the Feds!"

The two detectives standing on the porch looked at
each other with raised eyebrows, trying to figure out
what was going on. In the alley at the rear, Tevebaugh
and Osborne had just pulled their car up to the back of
the house when they saw a man carrying a revolver jump
out a rear window. One of the detectives quickly got
onto his radio and shouted, "He's going out a window!
Watch it, he's got a gun!"

As all four detectives headed off in pursuit, yelling
into their radios about the armed man's direction of
travel, the fleeing man leaped over a chain-link fence and
ran across a neighbor's yard, then leaped over the fence
on the other side. The officers had no idea who the man
was or why he was running. Still, they went after him,
figuring that he was likely wanted for *something*—why
else would he run? A couple of the detectives jumped
over the fence and tried to catch up with him, but the
officers soon lost the man in the neighborhood of closely
packed houses, which the runner clearly knew better
than they did.

The detectives immediately asked for assistance in setting up a security perimeter. Within minutes, uniformed officers and canine teams responded and quickly set one up, hoping to trap the fleeing man inside it. Detective Chris Smith called the Homicide Branch and told the detective who answered what had happened, describing the man who had fled from them.

"Damn, that was probably Brian Reese," the homicide detective replied. "He's the one we're looking for. We think he's probably involved in at least three murders."

Detective Smith tried to control his anger that Homicide hadn't mentioned anything about Brian Reese when they asked the detectives to go pick up Reese's girlfriend Lona Bishop. Even though Detective Cook hadn't known that Brian would be there, Detective Smith was still upset, because if he'd been aware that there was a possibility that a dangerous murder suspect might be at the address, he and the other three detectives would have handled the situation differently. They would have set up surveillance first and taken other safety precautions. But mostly, Detective Smith was upset because of how vulnerable he and the other detective had been when they walked up onto the porch of the house. They hadn't expected anything out of the ordinary, and had been left completely unprepared for the direction events took. They had simply gone to pick up Lona Bishop and bring her down to the Homicide Branch for an interview. Instead, they had ended up facing an armed murder suspect.

The uniformed officers who had been called to the scene, and who would keep the security perimeter up for two and a half hours, also became upset when they weren't told by the dispatchers until over an hour into manning the security perimeter that they were looking for an armed murder suspect. After being at the perimeter for a little over an hour, and as yet receiving no information about the person they were looking for other than his description, Sergeant Rick Snyder sent an officer to ask what the situation involved. Only then did the officers find out they were hunting for an armed murder suspect.

Regardless, neither the narcotics detectives, nor the uniformed officers manning the perimeter, nor the canine officers could find any sign of Brian Reese. (They would later learn that he had hidden for a short time in a burned-out and abandoned house in the neighborhood. While there, Brian found some old, raggedy clothing and came up with a plan for how to get out of the neighborhood. He changed into the clothing he found, smeared some of the soot from the house onto his face and arms, then left the abandoned house and walked down an alley, opening trash cans and looking in them. By so doing, Brian was able to walk unchallenged out of the neighborhood disguised as a homeless person, not an unusual sight for the area. He hid the revolver he had been carrying in a trash can near the abandoned house.) While the officers were disappointed that they weren't able to locate the fleeing man, this wasn't the first person to ever escape from the police, so, after a thorough search of the neighborhood, the security perimeter was finally taken down after two and a half hours.

Several homicide detectives went to 215 North Hamilton Avenue and talked with Lona Bishop, a thin woman in her early twenties with long, dark hair. Lona at first denied that the man who had run from the police was Brian Reese. Even though she and Brian had a child together, she insisted that the man who ran was another man she was dating named Steven Fillipo. The detectives also found Lona's mother, Rosemary Bishop, in the house, and she told the officers that the man who fled was Brian Reese. Eventually, Lona also admitted that it had been Brian, and that the two of them, as well as Brian's father, Paul Reese Sr., had been smoking crack cocaine that day. As a consequence, she said, Brian had been extremely hyper. That was likely why he'd been spooked by the detectives' arrival.

Following the failed attempt to apprehend Brian Reese on North Hamilton Avenue, the homicide detectives tried to anticipate where he would go next. They figured that Brian likely wouldn't come back to Lona's house, so he only had a few other options. (The police would later discover, however, that Brian did return to the area. After he'd left in the disguise of a homeless person, he went to a friend's house, then had that friend drive him back to the Hamilton Street area so that he could see what the police were up to, and so that he could recover the revolver he had hidden in the trash can.) The homicide detectives knew that, along with his child with Lona, Brian also had three other children with another woman, named Amy Brackin, but they figured he wouldn't go to her because she had since married another man. Lona told the police that Brian would probably go to his mother for help. And so, the homicide detectives asked Detective Jeff Wood of the Violent Crimes Unit to set up surveillance on Brian's mother, Barbara Reese.

Like many others in the Reese family, Barbara had a criminal record and had been suspected, though never charged, with assisting her ex-husband and four sons in their numerous criminal exploits. A few hours after Detective Wood began his surveillance of Barbara Reese at her house on North Bosart Street, he followed her as she left her home in a white minivan and drove over to the Little Flower Catholic Church in the 4700 block of East 13th Street. A few moments after she pulled into the parking lot of the church, Detective Wood found that Homicide's hunch had been right: Brian came running out of the building and jumped into the waiting van.

As the van pulled away from the church, Wood put out an alert on the police radio and told the dispatcher that he was following a murder suspect in a white minivan heading south on North Linwood Avenue toward East 10th Street. Uniformed officers Jason Fishburn and Jerry Piland, who were nearby, heard the radio broadcast and raced over to position their cars at 10th and Linwood, preparing to intercept the van. However, instead of stopping for the police cars, Barbara sped around them, and the police began pursuing her. She headed south on Linwood Avenue toward the east border of the Linwood Square Shopping Center.

After about a block or so, Barbara swerved the van into the parking lot of the shopping center and then slammed on the brakes in front of a Kroger's supermarket. As soon as the van stopped, Brian leaped out and started running. Although the officers didn't know it, he was again carrying the revolver. The officers who had been in pursuit of the minivan radioed that Brian was headed south on foot from the Kroger's parking lot. A few moments later, he disappeared behind the Kroger's building.

Officer Jason Fishburn could see Brian running south of the Kroger's so he drove his car into the Linwood Square Apartments complex, just south of the shopping center, in an effort to cut Brian off. At the south end of the apartment area, Fishburn jumped out of his police car and started in pursuit on foot, being the person closest to Brian. Fishburn was twenty-nine years old, lean, and in excellent shape, and he soon began to catch up with Brian, who was thirty-six and a heavy drug user, which seldom enhances a person's health. Several other officers also joined in the foot pursuit but were several seconds behind Fishburn.

"Stop! Police!" Fishburn shouted as he got closer to Brian, apparently not seeing the revolver he carried.

While the other officers took off in foot pursuit of Brian, two officers stayed on the scene to arrest Barbara Reese on charges of resisting law enforcement and obstructing justice. An officer said in his arrest report that "she stated her son had told her that he was on the run." She also told the officer that she had intended to take Brian to her house at 1428 North Bosart Street but changed her mind when she saw several police officers in the neighborhood. She would later be convicted of resisting law enforcement and receive a six-month jail sentence.

Meanwhile, Fishburn, who saw that Brian didn't intend to stop and surrender voluntarily, made a quick tactical decision when he was about ten feet or so behind the runner. Rather than using his pistol, Fishburn instead pulled out his Taser and fired it at Brian. But the Taser's metal prongs missed the man, who leaped over a guardrail at the south edge of the apartment area and went through a gap in a privacy fence just beyond it, then ran south in the 800 block of North Euclid Avenue.

Later, during all of the debriefings and tactical discussions of the incident, the question would arise of why, since Fishburn knew that he was chasing a murder suspect, he would attempt to use his Taser rather than his pistol, which would have been legal and proper to use since Brian was a dangerous fleeing felon. While some might argue that it's always best to try to arrest someone in the most humane way possible, a decision like Fishburn's often has more to do with wanting to avoid the months and months of red tape and hell that follows any officer-involved shooting, even if that shooting is perfectly legal, as it would have been in this case.

It's standard procedure in a police shooting for the officers involved to be removed from regular duties and put on desk duty somewhere, often for months. The officers will then have to appear and testify before the firearms review board and a grand jury. They know that they will also often be scrutinized and criticized in the press by various human rights groups, and judged by individuals who will have weeks and months to study the decision that they made in a split second. Individuals who study these events from a quiet, calm distance often don't realize how frantic and confusing these events can be as they are unfolding, and how quickly these life-or-death decisions have to be made. Therefore, most officers avoid using their guns if at all possible, even though it often puts their own lives at risk.

Regardless though of why Officer Fishburn decided to attempt using his Taser, it didn't work, and because of his attempt to deploy it, he found that he had lost ground on Brian and had to race to catch up. Nevertheless, due to his youth and speed, Fishburn still outdistanced the other officers and quickly began to catch up again with Brian Reese, who suddenly disappeared around the corner of a house at 810 North Euclid Avenue.

When Fishburn turned the corner and ran into the narrow space between 810 and the house to the south, Brian was waiting behind a cutout on the house at 810 and fired at him with the .38 caliber revolver he carried. The first shot struck Fishburn in the lower abdomen, and though painful, was not incapacitating, since he wore a bulletproof vest. Fishburn dropped the Taser he still held in his hand and immediately pulled out his .40 caliber Glock semiautomatic pistol. Before the officer could get a shot off, however, the next shot from Brian struck him in the left side of the head. Fishburn fired a shot in return, but it went uselessly into the dirt in front of him as he dropped to the ground, critically wounded. Brian, seeing the officer down, turned and ran back out onto Euclid Avenue.

Three of the other officers involved in the foot chase of Brian Reese—Detective Jeff Wood, Detective Steve Scott, and Patrol Officer Jerry Piland—reached the 800 block of North Euclid Avenue seconds after Fishburn. They had heard the gunshots but didn't know what had happened. Sergeant Rick Snyder, Officer Brian Mack, and Officer Greg Crabtree also began closing in on the scene. Suddenly, the officers saw Brian Reese appear from between two houses. When Brian Reese saw the officers, he raised the revolver he carried and pointed it at them. Detectives Wood and Scott fired their own weapons at him, one of the shots striking Brian in the left shoulder. Brian ran around a nearby house but then went down, the fight out of him. When the officers rushed up to Brian to secure his weapon, they found him bleeding profusely, and one of the officers called on his radio for medical help.

As the officers handcuffed Brian, Sergeant Snyder began counting heads, making sure everyone was accounted for. He found he was short one.

Just then, one of the officers said, "Where's Fish? I can't find Fish."

The officers all looked at one another then started off in the direction they had seen Brian Reese come from. The first thing they saw were the soles of Officer Jason Fishburn's shoes as he lay on the ground. The officers ran up to him but didn't see his head wound because of the way he was lying. He wasn't unconscious, but he wasn't totally alert, either. His breathing, the officers noticed, sounded painful and labored. They immediately began cutting off his shirt when they saw the bullet hole in it. They also took off his bulletproof vest and found a large, dark bruise on his stomach. One of the officers shouted that he'd found the bullet still encased in the bulletproof vest. Everyone relaxed. Fishburn's funny breathing was just because he'd had the wind knocked out of him.

Just then, Fishburn turned his head and the officers saw the huge wound to the left side of it. Sergeant Snyder knew that he had to do something quickly. Fortunately, Officer Greg Crabtree had been a medic in the military, and after becoming a police officer he had assembled a gunshot response bag that he equipped with the same medical equipment he had used to treat battlefield gunshot wounds. Crabtree grabbed the bag from his car and began stabilizing and prepping Fishburn for the ride to the hospital.

Indianapolis Metropolitan Police Department sergeant Dennis Fishburn, Jason's father, would later call Crabtree's preparedness "the real miracle about that day."

"That's not normal equipment that we carry around," he said. "We were lucky that they were able to prep him on the scene so that when the ambulance got there he was ready to go."

Sergeant Snyder, confident that Fishburn was getting the best medical care possible at the moment, turned his mind to other tactical matters. The ambulance would have to be able to get through to the scene, which was now clogged with police cars. He immediately got the cars moved and made a path for the ambulance. Fortunately, an ambulance had heard about the chase on their radio and had decided to head that way just in case they were needed, but even though Sergeant Snyder had cleared the police cars out of the way, the ambulance still found its path blocked by a civilian car. Knowing that the officer needed help as quickly as possible, the ambulance driver managed to use the ambulance to push the car out of the way. Consequently, they were at the scene within minutes, and luckily, since Officer Crabtree had already stabilized and prepped Fishburn, all the ambulance driver and med tech needed to do was load him into the ambulance.

Although Sergeant Snyder had intended to stay behind and manage the crime scene, the ambulance driver and med tech requested that he ride in the back with Officers Fishburn and Piland. So Snyder turned the crime scene over to another sergeant and climbed into the back of the ambulance. Throughout the ride, Sergeant Snyder continuously encouraged Fishburn to hang on, telling him over and over that he was going to be okay. He kept telling him, "Not today! Not today!"

There was reason to be hopeful. Less than three years earlier, Officer Michael Antonelli of the Indianapolis Metropolitan Police Department had also sustained a gunshot to the head, in his case one where the bullet exited out his right eye. Although that incident had appeared grave at the scene, Officer Antonelli not only survived the injury but returned to the police department eight months after the incident. Situations like this, Sergeant Snyder knew, weren't totally hopeless.

Along with offering encouragement, Sergeant Snyder also performed another critical task while in the back of the ambulance. Getting on his police radio, he had several police cars that were already accompanying them block all of the major cross streets along the route so that the ambulance could get to Wishard Memorial Hospital as quickly as possible. The police department helicopter, Air One, was up that day, and also able to scout the best route to the hospital and advise the ground units where traffic needed to be stopped. Officer Piland helped by getting the oxygen line working and assisting with other emergency matters. Fishburn seemed to understand the grave condition he was in, and used his left hand to hold his eyes open in an apparent attempt to not lose consciousness.

A look at the communications log for July 10, 2008, shows that, amazingly, only twenty-three minutes passed between the start of the incident, when Detective Wood requested assistance in stopping Barbara Reese's van at 7:17 P.M., to the arrival of Officer Jason Fishburn at Wishard Memorial Hospital at 7:40 P.M., a trip of over five miles to the west of Euclid Avenue. The doctors there credited the speed of arrival—from the time Fishburn was loaded into the ambulance to the time he arrived was eleven minutes—and the care he had received on the scene as being responsible for Fishburn's condition when he reached the hospital. Most people with similar head wounds didn't arrive alive.

Fortunately for Officer Jason Fishburn, despite his arrival during shift change at the hospital, the staff there had heard that a police officer had been shot and was en route. Most of the staff had stayed on in order to give the officer the best care possible. Sergeant Snyder said that as they wheeled Fishburn into the hospital, he saw the hallway lined with doctors and nurses, already masked and gloved, and ready to go.

Meanwhile, as all of this was occurring, Detective Sergeant Jeff Breedlove of the Homicide Branch sat in an interrogation room at police headquarters conducting an interview in a case unrelated to the Fishburn shooting. But he was the detective next in rotation, which meant he received the shooting of Officer Jason Fishburn as his investigation.

Crimes like this one are naturally extremely emotional for other officers, and as a consequence, dozens of police officers will often respond to the scene. Detective Sergeant Breedlove knew this could result in serious contamination of the crime scene, so he left the Homicide Office immediately, even before Officer Fishburn made it to the hospital. In fact, Breedlove recalled seeing the ambulance with Fishburn en route to Wishard Memorial Hospital fly by him as he drove to the crime scene, about four miles east of police headquarters.

Breedlove knew that homicide detectives on another shift had been looking at Brian Reese for at least one and possibly three murders. But that was all he knew about Brian Reese at the time, who was at that same moment also in an ambulance en route to Wishard Memorial Hospital.

The crime scene, Detective Sergeant Breedlove discovered upon his arrival, was huge, extending from 1400 North Bosart Avenue down to 810 North Euclid Avenue, over a half mile long and a quarter mile wide. Unfortunately, as often happens with crime scenes like this, there had been a lot of traffic in and out of it.

"The crime scene wasn't the way we like it because there were too many people trampling around in it," Detective Sergeant Breedlove recalled. "A crime scene is never as perfect as we'd like it to be, but [in this case] there was a lot of evidence lying around, shell casings and all, and people were walking on them. It was pretty chaotic because the crime scene went all the way from Bosart Street down to where the shooting took place. That was a lot of area to try to cover."

Detective Sergeant Breedlove did the best he could with the crime scene he had. Even so, there were several shell casings that should have been there that he couldn't find.

"We took a metal detector out there to try and find the shell casings, but we didn't have much luck," he said. "The yards in that neighborhood have so much metal, trash, and stuff that's been thrown around there that the metal detector just went off constantly. It really didn't do us any good."

However, Detective Sergeant Breedlove was able to retrieve the .38 caliber revolver Brian Reese had used to shoot Officer Fishburn, and found that it contained five spent rounds and one live one in the cylinder. He also recovered Officer Fishburn's .40 caliber Glock, his Taser, and other important evidence. But at any shooting scene where there are unaccounted-for shots fired, the homicide detective always tries to find out where these shots went to.

"We looked everywhere for bullet holes at the crime scene where Fishburn had been shot," said Breedlove. "I went back several times looking for bullet holes in the houses and all, but we never found any." This would eventually become a crucial point undermining the defense attorney's later claim that his client hadn't meant to kill Officer Fishburn when he fired the revolver at him, but had just shot blindly in his direction. If that had been the case, they ought to have found bullets other than only those two that had hit Officer Fishburn.

The upside to having so many detectives respond to the crime scene and offer their assistance was that Detective Sergeant Breedlove had plenty of officers available to canvass the neighborhood around the crime scene. He hoped to find someone in the neighborhood who might have seen what happened between Officer Fishburn and Brian Reese. At that moment, no one felt certain that Fishburn would survive his wounds, and Breedlove figured that Reese would probably lawyer up and not talk. It would be great to have an outside witness to the incident. Unfortunately, though, while a lot of people had witnessed the chase, no one saw the actual shooting of Officer Fishburn.

"From the canvass we had an eight-year-old girl who said she saw the shooting through a window," said Breedlove. "I went and spoke with her and found out that what she had witnessed was the shooting of Brian Reese by the police officers, rather than Officer Fishburn's shooting. I took some photographs from where she said she saw the shooting just to be certain of what she could have seen."

Despite Brian Reese's own shooting at the crime scene, he wasn't gravely injured himself, and the hospital released him later that night. The police brought him down to the Homicide Office for questioning. Detective Sergeant Breedlove went into an interrogation room to question him and had him sign a Miranda rights waiver. But the interview didn't get very far.

"Reese kept closing his eyes and saying he wanted to take a nap," said Breedlove. "I was kind of worried about how much medicine he was on and how much it affected him." Consequently, he stopped the interview before it even started.

Breedlove finally left the Homicide Office at around 4:00 A.M. His pregnant wife had an appointment for an ultrasound at 8:00 A.M., so he took her to it and then returned to the Homicide Office at around 10:00 A.M.

"When I walked in the Homicide Office I saw that the mayor and the chief of police were there," said Breedlove. "The captain asked me to go in and see if Brian wanted to talk."

Surprisingly, Detective Sergeant Breedlove found that Brian was still in the interview room and was now fully aware of what was going on. "I went back to talk to Brian Reese and he said that he'd talk if we got him some cigarettes and food," said Breedlove. "I didn't want to do that because I knew it would have caused all kinds of problems with the case, and I really didn't need to talk to him anyway. So I just ordered a wagon and had him taken over to the jail."

Months later in the investigation, Detective Sergeant Breedlove would receive a letter sent by a prison inmate named Gary Rees, who claimed that he had befriended Brian while in a holding cell waiting for court and that Brian had told him the real story about what happened with Officer Fishburn. Detectives get many of these types of offers to help, but many turn out to be simply individuals willing to say anything if they think it will help to reduce their sentence. Breedlove knew that he would have to notify the Prosecutor's Office about this and then check out Gary Rees's story thoroughly.

Meanwhile, the previous evening at Wishard Memorial Hospital, dozens of fellow police officers, including high-ranking ones, had rushed to the hospital to show their concern and support for Jason Fishburn. Chief of police Michael Spears told the news media, "Officer Fishburn is our hero. [He] was out there doing everything the citizens of this city want from its police department. He was out there fighting for a victim who couldn't fight for himself, for a sixty-nine-year-old man [Clifford Haddix] who was brutally and savagely and cowardly murdered within his own home."

Upon Officer Fishburn's arrival at Wishard Memorial Hospital, the staff had immediately wheeled him into one of the shock rooms. The doctors at the hospital went right to work, but after examining Fishburn's injuries, they didn't see much chance for his survival. The bullet wound was deep and massive. "The majority of people who have a gunshot wound to the brain do not survive," Dr. Richard Rogers, one of the treating physicians at Wishard Memorial Hospital, told the news media. He said that he didn't hold out much hope for Fishburn's survival.

After the doctors had examined Fishburn in the shock room, though, they realized that the fact he was still alive at all with such a massive head wound meant that he had an incredible will to live, and that just maybe they could save him. But they also realized that his only chance of survival lay in immediate surgery. The surgery required would be very risky, and the hospital needed an okay from his wife before they could start.

"I was driving home from work when I heard about Jason being shot," said Tonya Fishburn, Jason's wife, an employee of the Marion County Crime Lab. "I was trying to get ahold of Jason because I saw a lot of police cars speeding by me. Then Dennis, Jason's father, called me. He told me that Jason had been shot and that I should get to Wishard Hospital right away."

Naturally, no one ever wants to receive such news. Although Tonya immediately started for the hospital, she was nearly overcome with panic and worry.

"I started toward Wishard Hospital, and of course I was pretty hysterical at the time," said Tonya. "One of the officers called me and told me to pull over, and then she drove me to the hospital."

The officer, who knew Fishburn's wife because of Tonya's job at the crime lab, sped to the hospital as quickly as she could. During the drive, the officer wanted to comfort and reassure Tonya, but it was hard under the circumstances—no one really knew how bad it was, or if her husband would even be alive when they arrived there. Once at the hospital, the officer took Tonya through the waiting room and into the emergency room, where the doctors had Officer Fishburn in Shock Room 4.

"It's kind of a blur, but there were just a lot of officers at the hospital," said Tonya. "It was almost overwhelming, the number of people there."

Jason's father, Dennis Fishburn, had already arrived at the hospital and was waiting there for Tonya. He had received a call from his brother Darin, who worked for the Fraternal Order of Police, and who told him to get to the hospital right away.

"I was visiting a friend from church when my cell phone went off," said Dennis Fishburn. "I stepped into the kitchen and answered it. It was Darin. He told me that he'd been in a meeting and heard about Jason's situation. So he left the meeting to give me the bad news. He told me that not only had Jason been shot, but that he had been shot in the head. It was a terrible phone call. Just one you don't want to get, not knowing the outcome." Dennis, a sergeant at the Indianapolis Metropolitan Police Department, had been a police officer for a long time. He knew how devastating gunshot wounds to the head could be.

After calling his daughter-in-law Tonya, Dennis made another difficult phone call. "It was about 7:45 at night," said Dennis. "My wife was in Columbus, Ohio. Our [other] son, who is on the Columbus, Ohio, Police Department, and his wife had just given birth to their second child. My wife was there to help with our two-year-old granddaughter. So I had to give her a call, and she was able to drive back and meet us at Wishard Hospital later that night."

Following the two phone calls, Dennis sped to the hospital, expecting the worst.

"My first thoughts," said Dennis, "were that I would go to Wishard Hospital and they'd say that Jason had fought a valiant fight, that they'd done all they could, but that he had died."

But remarkably, Jason Fishburn was still alive.

It didn't take long for the news of Fishburn's shooting to reach the public safety community. Many police officers, firefighters, and other emergency workers, learning of the shooting and wanting to show their support, had rushed to Wishard Memorial Hospital. "When my daughter and I got to the hospital," Dennis said, "there was a sea of blue uniforms; there were police everywhere."

As the members of Officer Jason Fishburn's family arrived at Wishard Memorial Hospital, the staff put them in a special family waiting room. Along with Jason's wife and mother and father, many other relatives also showed up at the hospital, including in-laws, grandparents, and aunts and uncles. No one knew much about what had happened except that Fishburn had been shot in the head. They didn't know how serious his injury was, what his prognosis was, or what the doctors intended to do.

"Jason had gotten there before I did, and so we were all just waiting around for the doctors to come in, just waiting to hear how Jason was and what was going on," recalled Tonya.

Unfortunately, the doctors didn't have good news for the family. "Few people who suffer head wounds this serious survive," the doctors at Wishard Memorial Hospital told the family gathered there. "But if we're going to have any chance at all of saving him, he needs to go to surgery right now."

The head of the surgical team that would operate on Fishburn, Dr. Richard Rogers, was a member of Wishard Memorial Hospital's top neurosurgery team. An assistant professor of neurological surgery at the Indiana University School of Medicine, Dr. Rogers was also chief of surgery at Indiana University Health West Hospital. Yet even with all of his credentials and experience, Dr. Rogers didn't hold out much hope for Fishburn's survival.

"The majority of people who have a gunshot wound to the brain [like Officer Fishburn's] do not survive," Dr. Rogers told the news media, "so for the first twenty-four to forty-eight hours or so, our goal is to do everything to allow that patient to survive that injury." The gunshot wound to the left side of his head was described as "devastating." Fishburn had also suffered a gunshot wound to the lower abdomen, though that impact had largely been absorbed by the bulletproof vest he wore.

"The doctors came in pretty quickly after Tonya had gotten there," said Dennis Fishburn. "Dr. Rogers told us that Jason was critically injured and that they didn't know if he was going to make it or not. The doctor said that Jason had to have surgery right away if he was going to have any chance at all of living. The doctor also said that he couldn't promise us that Jason would make it through the surgery. He said that they'd do their best, but without surgery Jason would certainly die. Dr. Rogers also told us that Jason's brain was swelling and that they had to get in there and not only clean up where the bullet had penetrated, but also take off that section of his cranium, the whole left side of his head, to allow his brain to expand. And if they didn't do that right away he would certainly die."

"The doctors told us that Jason had been shot in the head, and that his condition was extremely critical," said Tonya. "His father had wanted him to have a blessing first from our church, but the doctors said there was no time. They had to do surgery right away. Really, what I thought was that they were preparing us for the fact that he probably wouldn't survive the surgery. They said that most people with a wound like his didn't survive."

However, Dr. Rogers wasn't through yet with the bad news. "Dr. Rogers also said that even if Jason did make it through the operation, he still couldn't guarantee his recovery," Dennis said. "Many things could still go wrong. If he survived the surgery, the doctor said that

Jason would be put into an induced coma for at least forty-eight hours. They didn't want any movement at all from him. They would need him to be completely still. So Tonya signed the paperwork and off he went to surgery." The family all agreed that his fate was now in God's hands, and each said a prayer for him.

The family of Officer Fishburn, of course, was devastated by Dr. Rogers's prognosis but also knew that there was really no choice at all about having the surgery done. It was Fishburn's only chance. And he was young and in good health, which Dr. Rogers had said would help his odds. But even more important, because Fishburn had been transported to the hospital so quickly after the shooting, and had received such good trauma care on the scene, his chances were better than average. His brain hadn't had much time to swell, which is one of the leading causes of death with this type of injury.

There was nothing else the family could do but simply settle in for the long wait. But it wasn't an easy wait. And though all of the family members in the waiting room tried to keep up a brave face, in each of their minds they feared that at any moment the doctor would return and tell them that Jason Fishburn hadn't made it.

EIGHT

After being treated at the hospital for his shoulder injury, Brian Reese had been transported back to police headquarters, even though the staff at Wishard Memorial Hospital had given him some strong painkillers. After Brian sat all night in an interrogation room, the police sent him over to the Marion County Jail, just a block south of police headquarters. The Marion County Prosecutor's Office at this point wasn't sure what Brian would end up being charged with in the Fishburn shooting. Right now, the prosecutor could charge him with attempted murder, but the prognosis for Officer Jason Fishburn, they learned, was not good at all, and if Fishburn died, it would become murder. They decided to wait a bit. Brian wasn't going anywhere anyway, given all the other charges on him. His mother, Barbara Reese, also sat in jail, waiting for her first court appearance on the resisting law enforcement and obstruction of justice charges.

Meanwhile, back at Wishard Memorial Hospital, Officer Jason Fishburn's family prayed for him constantly, reflecting on what a good person he was. Before becoming a police officer at age twenty-four, Fishburn had spent two years as a missionary. He'd always been soft-hearted, and had twice brought home stray dogs he had encountered while on patrol.

The Fishburns were a law enforcement family. Not only did Jason's father, Dennis, also work for the Indianapolis Metropolitan Police Department, but his wife, Tonya, worked for the Marion County Crime Lab; his brother worked as a police officer in Columbus, Ohio; an uncle had retired after working as a deputy U.S. Marshal; an aunt was a retired police officer; and an aunt and uncle both worked for the local Fraternal Order of Police. Police families know that these sorts of things can happen, but still no one is really prepared for it—and it didn't make the waiting any easier.

After two and a half hours in surgery, Dr. Richard Rogers returned to the waiting room with good news for the Fishburn family: Jason had made it through the operation. Surgeons had had to remove part of Fishburn's skull in order to relieve the pressure from swelling, and because of this, and because he was now in such a fragile state, they had put Fishburn into an induced coma to help with his recovery. The doctor also warned that the next few days to a week would be critical to Fishburn's survival. He explained to them that Fishburn had lost 10 percent of his brain to the gunshot and surgery, and that now there was a real danger of infection and blood clotting. The doctor warned the family to be prepared, because there were just so many things that could still go wrong.

"Dr. Rogers came back in and told us that Jason had made it through the surgery," said Dennis, Jason Fishburn's father. "He said that the next forty-eight hours would be extremely critical to his survival, but that he could not give us any guarantee as to whether Jason would make it or not, only time would tell. They'd done all they could do at present."

But even with Dr. Rogers's warning, Fishburn's family couldn't help but believe that a miracle had happened. No matter what the doctor said about Fishburn's chances of survival, the family now had some real hope.

During a press conference later at the hospital, Dr. Rogers gave much of the same news to the public. "We want people to be cautiously optimistic, but not give people false hope," he said.

Like Fishburn's family, his fellow police officers couldn't help but also believe that a miracle was possible. A police department spokesperson told the news media that "[Fishburn] hasn't given up, so we aren't abandoning hope."

On the day following the operation, Dr. Rogers and several other physicians on the surgical team held another press conference. Dr. Rogers told those attending it that he and his team were now cautiously optimistic about Fishburn's survival, but also warned that many things could still go wrong. "His condition is still guarded," Dr. Gerardo Gomez, director of Wishard Memorial Hospital's Level I Trauma Center, told those at the press conference. "Our main concern is survival."

Dennis asked those at the news conference to pray for his son. "I am a firm believer in the power of prayer," he said. He believed that prayer had helped his son survive the operation, and would also help him make a recovery.

The night before, Greg Ballard, the mayor of Indianapolis, had been attending the opening ceremonies for the Indiana Black Expo, which were being held at the Light of the World Christian Church, when he learned of Officer Fishburn's shooting. He told the gathering about it and said, "It doesn't look good." Also that night, a group of citizens, after learning of the incident, organized a prayer vigil on the parking lot of the Linwood Square Shopping Center, where the foot chase had begun. The dozens who attended this impromptu service prayed for Fishburn's survival and for his family.

On this night, a local church organized a prayer vigil outside the hospital, which scores of people attended, and several hundred people also showed up for a blood drive organized in Fishburn's name. All of Fishburn's family members prayed that the miracle wouldn't end.

Because of Fishburn's precarious state, his family camped out at the hospital as he remained in the medically induced coma.

"It kind of felt like the whole world had stopped," Tonya recalled. "Your whole world existed right there in that hospital room. They told us not to pay any attention to the monitors or anything else going on, but you couldn't help it. Anytime his blood pressure alarm went off I stopped breathing, and couldn't breathe again until the alarm had stopped. I was constantly on edge, doing a lot of praying. I kind of lost track of time. I didn't know if it was day or night. I was in my own little world worrying about Jason."

Fortunately, Fishburn's family received a tremendous amount of support. As the family waited at the hospital, members of the church the Fishburns attended sent food to the hospital for them, and even mowed their lawn so that the family wouldn't have to leave the hospital. "The support Jason received was phenomenal," said his father. "Lots of members of our church showed up and so did a lot of police officers. I remember that for several days there was just a constant sea of blue uniforms in the hospital. The chief of police visited us, the public safety director visited us, and even the mayor came. The mayor usually travels with a security detail, and the first time he visited us he came with them. But there were a couple of times that he and his wife would come early in the morning or late at night without his security. They would come and sit and talk with us for a while."

But despite the support, Dennis had a tough time initially. "The first few days really took a toll on me. When I first got there I thought I'd be told that my son had died. When I did get there and heard the circumstances of what had happened I started getting really angry. I knew that the suspect who had shot my son had been in that same hospital. And I have to tell you, I had some bad feelings toward that individual, even to the point where I said I'd like to have five minutes alone with him for what he had done to my son.

"I became full of anger," Dennis went on, "full of hate for the man who had shot my son. But around 5:00 A.M. the morning after Jason had come out of the surgery, I was still thinking about Brian Reese. And suddenly I knew that I didn't have a good relationship with God. I was thinking too much about my hatred for the man who had shot Jason. So I went down to the hospital chapel and I prayed. I realized that I had to let go of the hate. The only way to help Jason was to clear my mind of it. I felt that God wanted us to be strong. He would make the decision as to whether Jason would make it or not, and whatever that decision would be, it'd be in God's hands, and we'd accept it.

"Jason and I have always had a great relationship, and my wife and I and Tonya were at the hospital all day every day," continued Dennis. "We took courage in Jason's fight. It helped us stay strong. I felt that Jason could hear us. I don't know if that's medically true or not, but we always spoke to him, talked to him, encouraged him. We kept telling him that he was going to be all right."

On Saturday, July 12, 2008, two days after the shooting, hundreds of people attended another prayer vigil held outside the hospital. Indianapolis mayor Greg Ballard addressed the crowd and thanked them for their support of Officer Fishburn. Near the same time, Fishburn's family reported what they saw as significant progress. Even though Jason was still in the induced coma, they noticed movement in his eyes and fingers, and they said that he raised his left hand slightly when his mother touched him. A friend who had visited Fishburn at the hospital also told the news media that Fishburn had tried to remove some tape on his arm that was apparently bothering him. The family couldn't help but be encouraged.

After three days, the doctors took Fishburn out of the induced coma but warned that even though things looked optimistic, many, many things could still go wrong—at any moment Fishburn could die suddenly from a number of different causes. "The doctors told us that they still had worries about infection, pneumonia, blot clots, and a dozen other things that could go wrong," said Dennis. "They said that there were still all kinds of things they had to be very careful about." The doctors told them that Fishburn's condition was too delicate to guarantee anything.

In addition to having to worry about the doctors' dire warnings, Fishburn's family could also see clear evidence of how badly the gunshot wound had affected his body. "Once they took him out of the induced coma, we watched him move, and noticed that all he could move was mostly his left side. He could move his right leg a little, but his right arm was dormant, didn't move at all," said Dennis.

Despite the doctors' cautions, Fishburn refused to give up and continued to show signs of improvement. Once he had passed the seventy-two-hour mark, during which time most patients with this type of massive head wound die, the doctors changed their focus to recovery, though they warned that it would still be long and difficult. No one knew yet the true extent of the injury Fishburn had suffered and how much it would affect his recovery.

On Wednesday, July 16, 2008, Fishburn pulled out his breathing tube, which had apparently been bothering him, and, to everyone's surprise, began breathing on his own. Several of the therapists who worked with Fishburn said that he continued to show very good progress.

But just one day later, on Thursday, July 17, 2008, a week after the shooting, surgeons had to rush Fishburn back into the operating room to remove liquids from his brain that had pooled there after his original surgery.

Yet still, Jason Fishburn persevered and hung on, defying the odds by living. Every day he seemed to get just a little bit better. Just over two weeks after the shooting Fishburn spoke his first words: "Oh my God, I want to go fishing," he told his family. He also told his wife that he loved her. Later, he recited the alphabet and counted for the therapists who had been working with him. Despite this progress, however, he had memory problems surrounding the incident that had landed him in the hospital. He didn't know why he was there.

"A couple weeks after the incident Jason looked at me and wanted to talk," said Dennis Fishburn. "He said, 'Dad, tell me what happened.' He wanted to know how he got there, and so I told him, 'Jason, you were chasing a homicide suspect, and you went between two homes, and he shot you. One of them was in the head, and you are in very critical condition. So you need to fight.' That was a very tough moment."

"His memory wasn't very good, so he would keep asking us what had happened, and we'd have to keep telling him," agreed Tonya. "We'd have to keep telling him why he was in the hospital. I'm sure it was a really frustrating time for him. I mean you wake up and you don't remember anything, just that you're in a hospital; you're in a hospital and you can't move part of your body."

Finally, on July 28, 2008, after Fishburn had been in the intensive care unit for over two weeks, the doctors at Wishard Memorial Hospital decided that he was well enough to be transferred to a rehabilitation center. The doctors had had to rebuild Fishburn's skull with a prosthetic because of the damage from the gunfire and surgery, but remarkably, it had worked without any serious complications. Fishburn had surpassed all of their expectations, first for survival and then for recovery, but he still had a long road ahead of him; even though he had survived the massive head wound, he had lost much of the feeling in his right side and couldn't use his right arm or leg. He would need a lot of professional rehabilitative therapy before he would be self-sufficient and mobile. But no amount of rehabilitation therapy would ever get him back to his pre-shooting state. He had suffered too much damage.

His family, though, believed that God had a plan. "We kept encouraging him," said Dennis. "We told him that a whole lot of people were praying for him. We told him that he was going to make it through this."

Since Officer Fishburn had been shot in the line of duty, the Indianapolis Metropolitan Police Department paid for all of his care and had him transferred to the Rehabilitation Hospital of Indiana, one of the top hospitals in the state for rehabilitation therapy. Nine weeks after his admittance there, the hospital released Fishburn to go home, something the doctors at Wishard Memorial Hospital would have thought impossible the night the officer was brought in. While Fishburn was still not functioning close to a hundred percent, the rehab therapists felt that they had done all they could for him as an inpatient. Although Fishburn required a brace on his right leg in order to walk, he refused assistance when leaving the facility. He told staff that he wanted to do it on his own—and then walked, very slowly, to the waiting car. As Fishburn left the hospital, his supervisor at the shooting scene several months earlier, Sergeant Rick Snyder, got on the police radio and said that one of his officers was still unaccounted for. Fishburn then got on the police radio and marked back into service, telling the dispatcher that he was going home.

Officer Fishburn's fight, however, wasn't over yet. He still needed to do a lot of work once he returned home in order to regain his physical strength and movement. It took day after day and month after month of intense physical therapy. And while he made significant improvement, he was still far from where he'd been before July 10, 2008. Fishburn longed to return to work as a police officer, a job he loved, and he knew he had a long, long way to go. But still he was determined to do it.

"Jason's recovery was really long," said Tonya. "He had a lot of physical therapy. He was in ICU for almost three weeks, and then he spent another nine weeks at the Rehabilitation Hospital. And even after that, for seven or eight months, he went to outpatient physical therapy three or four days a week."

The administration of the Indianapolis Metropolitan Police Department kept in contact with the Fishburn family and received regular updates on Jason's improvement. A year after the shooting, Indianapolis chief of police Michael Spears sent a letter to all employees of the Indianapolis Metropolitan Police Department, reminding them of Officer Fishburn's sacrifice and making sure he wasn't forgotten about.

The Indianapolis Metropolitan Police Department awarded Jason Fishburn a Purple Heart and also its highest award for valor: the Medal of Honor. The night the Rehabilitation Hospital of Indiana released Fishburn, he and his family attended an Indiana Fever WNBA basketball game. The audience gave him a standing ovation when he was introduced. Fishburn also became a finalist for the All-Star Award, given by the popular television program *America's Most Wanted*. And at ceremonies for National Police Week, held in April 2009 in Washington DC, Fishburn stepped forward to add a red carnation to the wreath for fallen police officers, the carnation meant to represent all disabled officers. Organizers held the ceremony at the memorial for police officers killed in the line of duty, a fate Fishburn had thankfully avoided.

Fishburn's condition kept improving, going against all

of the dire predictions the doctors had made when they first saw him at Wishard Memorial Hospital. While he could walk with the help of a leg brace, he still couldn't use his right arm. Since he was right-handed before the shooting, Fishburn had to teach himself to write with his left hand. But still, he wanted to try to return to police work. It was a job he had loved. And he improved so much that by May 18, 2009, he was able to return to work at the police department. The department assigned him to a light-duty position at the Training Academy, and he started off working four hours a day, four days a week, performing mostly administrative tasks.

"What we're trying to do is get him acclimated back into a work environment and assist him in his rehabilitation process," Indianapolis Metropolitan Police Department spokesperson Sergeant Paul Thompson told the news media.

"I think Jason is a miracle," says his wife Tonya. "He's a survivor. When he was at the hospital they were trying to prepare us for the worst, that he might not live, or that he might be comatose forever. But he surpassed all of their expectations in his recovery. I think that says a lot about his determination. As soon as he got out of the hospital he was ready to go back to work."

Dennis Fishburn also weighed in on how everything that happened to Jason affected his family. "In some ways this has been a blessing. I know that's hard to understand, but we've come through the deepest, darkest despair and abyss of life that can be imagined. You've got a son, not knowing if he is going to live or die, and to see the great miracle, to see God make his decision for Jason to pull through, it was all very miraculous.

"Jason has done everything to pay it forward," Dennis continued. "Since the shooting Jason has done a lot of community work. He works at a church food distribution center, goes out with the church missionaries, and visits with people who need help. He also does everything he can to keep his body in shape. He works out regularly at the YMCA. But sometimes still, even after witnessing it all, you can't help but wonder why one person lives and another dies. Jason's wound was the type most people don't survive. We have all thought about it a lot, and prayed about it a lot. We decided that there has to be a reason that Jason survived from this terrible, ugly mess. We believe that God's hand was there when Jason was shot, and that God prepared him for this great miracle. Jason obviously has something really important left to do."

Fishburn himself had one thing he wanted to say about everything he went through, and how it affected his outlook on life: "Don't live in the past," he said. "You've got to just move on."

Part of this moving on, of course, included bringing closure to the shooting incident. And so, once Fishburn had been released from outpatient therapy and returned to work at the police department, he decided that he wanted to attend the trial of the man who had shot him. Although he still couldn't recall any of the events of the day he was shot, or even remember anything at all about going to work that day, Fishburn made the decision that he not only wanted to attend the trial of Brian Reese, but that he also wanted to testify at it. And so, in November 2009, when the court scheduled Brian Reese to stand trial for the shooting incident, Fishburn stood ready to testify.

NINE

On July 31, 2008 (more than a year before the trial would begin and three days after Officer Jason Fishburn had been admitted to the Rehabilitation Hospital of Indiana), the Marion County Prosecutor's Office formally charged Brian Reese for the shooting of Officer Jason Fishburn. They charged him with attempted murder, carrying a handgun without a license, and resisting arrest. The Prosecutor's Office also said that it had not yet decided whether to seek the death penalty in the three murders Brian had also been accused of.

Brian Reese's trial for the attempted murder of Officer Jason Fishburn finally began on Monday, November 2, 2009. Fishburn had hung on to life so tenuously, and had made such a slow, yet remarkable, recovery, that the case had been in the Indianapolis news constantly. He'd become a local hero, and there had been dozens of newspaper articles and television news segments about the incident.

Due to the extensive pretrial publicity this case had received, Reese's attorney, public defender David Shircliff, didn't feel confident that they'd be able to find an unbiased jury of individuals in Indianapolis or the surrounding area who hadn't already heard story after story about the incident. Consequently, he filed for a change of venue and a judge ordered the trial moved to Valparaiso, Indiana, a small town of about 30,000 people, around 160 miles northwest of Indianapolis, near Chicago and Lake Michigan. Since the news in Valparaiso comes mainly from Chicago, not Indianapolis, most of the residents living there didn't know about the crime. Judge Lisa Borges of Indianapolis would preside at the trial, while Marion County prosecutor Carl Brizzi, assisted by deputy prosecutors Denise Robinson and Mark Hollingsworth, would handle the prosecution. Shircliff, the defense attorney, would be assisted by attorneys Laura Pitts and Jeffrey Neel.

For any victims of a serious crime, particularly those in which the victims have been seriously injured and permanently disabled, the trial of the person accused of committing that crime against them can be extremely emotional. The trauma of the trial can at times be nearly as bad as the trauma of the crime itself; the crime must be relived and talked about extensively. Victims who have often worked very hard to put the crime out of their thoughts and get on with their lives must now go through the whole thing again from the start. "I think there will be tender moments, some shedding of tears," Dennis Fishburn told a reporter for the Indy Channel. He said they could "expect an emotional rollercoaster as they relived tragic events in the courtroom."

Soon after his arrest, pictures of Brian Reese looking disheveled and angry had appeared over and over in the Indianapolis-area news media. But he cleaned up considerably for court; he didn't look anything like the scruffy man with the scowl in the mug shot taken right after his arrest. This was not unusual. Naturally, defense attorneys want their clients to play well to the jury, and so typically encourage their clients to look their best for court. Even Jason's father was taken aback by the change. "Reese looked very clean-cut during the trial," he said.

The first morning of the trial was spent selecting a jury. Prospective jurors underwent extensive questioning to be certain that they didn't know anything about the case or have any preconceived notions about it. As with the motivation behind the move from Indianapolis, the attorneys didn't want a jury full of people who'd already made their minds up about what had occurred.

Brian Reese's defense attorney David Shircliff had made this part of his questioning during voir dire, the process of questioning potential jurors for the purpose of finding those who can judge a case fairly. If during voir dire a person does show a problem that could affect his or her objectivity, that person can be removed from consideration as a juror. But while voir dire is meant to construct a jury that can be fair and impartial to both sides, the prosecutor and defense attorney actually use it for the opposite reason. What both really want is to get a jury that will be sympathetic to their side.

"Attorneys select jurors whom they will be able to persuade, not jurors who will be fair and impartial to both sides," said attorney Marni Becker-Avin in an article in the "Trial Techniques Committee newsletter," put out by the American Bar Association.

Fortunately, out of this group of potential jurors in Valparaiso, plenty of them hadn't heard about the case and felt that they could be unbiased, so the selection did not take long. Later that day, the judge swore in a jury of seven men and five women, with two women selected as alternate jurors, to be used in the event that any of the regular jurors could not complete the trial for some reason.

Even though the change to Valparaiso was a move made to benefit the defense, Detective Sergeant Jeff Breedlove, the homicide detective assigned to the case, felt it probably worked out just as well for the prosecution. He felt that the people in Porter County would likely be less sympathetic to Brian Reese's story. "They brought in about fifty potential jurors and I liked them all," he said. "I told the prosecutor that I'd take any twelve of them."

Shircliff also apparently felt that the selection of jurors had gone as well as possible for the defense. "All I can do is assume the jurors answered honestly, and I think they did," Shircliff told a reporter from WTHR Television. "The ones that are on the jury, I believe, said they could be fair and consider that the only intent for shooting a gun is not always to kill someone. It's possible you can shoot a gun without having that intent."

However, even after the jury had been selected, the defense attorney still faced a serious obstacle in this case: There was virtually no hope for a not guilty verdict. The defense could not deny that Brian Reese had shot Officer Fishburn. There were numerous witnesses who had seen Brian running with the revolver in his hand, witnesses who had heard the gunshots that struck Fishburn, and witnesses who had seen Brian running from the scene of the shooting. In addition, Brian had pointed the same gun Fishburn had been shot with at other police officers just before they shot him. The defense had no choice but to admit the shooting. Shircliff could only argue about Brian's intent when he did it. If the defense could convince the jury that Brian hadn't intended to kill Fishburn when he fired the gun at him, that he hadn't wanted to murder the police officer but only scare him, Brian's sentence would be much less severe. It was the defense's strategy to have the jury convict Brian of a lesser crime than attempted murder, such as aggravated battery.

The case, though difficult for the defense, wouldn't be a total slam dunk for the prosecution, either. The prosecution, of course, wanted a guilty verdict on the attempted murder charge but knew that it was not going to be an easy thing to get. "If you pull the trigger of a gun and someone dies as a result, that's murder, whether you intended that to happen or not," Marion County prosecutor Carl Brizzi told a reporter for WTHR. "With attempt murder you have to show intent to kill. That crime in Indiana is probably the most difficult crime to prove."

Deputy prosecutor Denise Robinson agreed. "Attempt Murder is the only specific intent crime in Indiana," she said. "In an attempt murder case, the prosecution is required to prove beyond a reasonable doubt that the defendant specifically intended to kill the victim. In my opinion, that makes attempt murder one of the most, if not the most, difficult charges to prove in this state."

By the time the prosecution and the defense had finished choosing a jury, it was already late afternoon, so Judge Lisa Borges decided there would be no testimony that day. Instead, she welcomed the jury and gave them their instructions about not talking to anyone about the case or watching or reading any news media stories about it. She also told the jurors that if during the trial they had a question they wanted to ask a witness, to write the question down and give it to the bailiff. The judge would read the question and then, if appropriate, she would ask the witness the question. She scheduled the testimony to begin the next day, Tuesday, November 3, 2009.

On Tuesday, before any testimony started, both sides got to give opening statements. The prosecution went first and told the jury that they would prove that Brian Reese had shot Officer Jason Fishburn with the intent to kill him. The defense then gave their opening statement, in which they said that what had happened on July 10, 2008, was simply a tragic accident, and that there had been no intent to kill Officer Fishburn.

Following the opening statements, the first witness the prosecution put on the stand was Officer Fishburn. He still had no recollection of the events of the day he was shot, but the prosecution wanted the jury to see and hear about the injuries he had suffered. Fishburn couldn't use his right arm, he walked only with the aid of a brace on his right leg, and he had difficulty with his speech. The prosecution wanted the jury to see that the injuries Fishburn had suffered weren't minor wounds that would heal over time, but lifelong disabilities. He told the jury about his memory lapse and that he presently worked at the Indianapolis Metropolitan Police Department Training Academy. Prosecutor Carl Brizzi asked him if he knew he was a police officer on July 10, 2008, and that he had been shot. He said yes.

Following his testimony, Fishburn went to sit with his wife in the courtroom audience. After the jury had been removed, Shircliff immediately objected to Fishburn's continued presence in court. He said that the constant reminder of the victim in the courtroom, especially since his injuries were now so apparent to the jury, would unfairly prejudice them against his client. In response to this, the prosecution presented case law that supported allowing Fishburn to remain in the courtroom, and consequently Judge Borges denied this objection but did have Jason and Tonya Fishburn sit where they wouldn't be in the jury's direct line of sight.

After Jason Fishburn's testimony, which hadn't taken long since the defense said it had no cross-examination, his wife Tonya next took the witness stand. She told the jurors that she worked at the Marion County Crime Lab, and that she and Jason had been married in June 2002. She then went on to talk about how the shooting had nearly destroyed her life. Tonya spoke about how the shooting had negatively affected both her and Fishburn's lives, about his slow recovery, and about how much things had changed in the lives of everyone in the Fishburn family since the event.

"What were the following days like for you?" Brizzi asked.

"They were the worst days of my life," she answered.

Again, the defense declined to cross-examine.

"I learned a lot at the trial," Tonya later said. "The trial was the first time I found out exactly what had happened the day Jason had been shot." But while enlightening, the criminal trial was also tiring and emotion filled. "The trial was long and stressful," said Tonya. And watching the accused perpetrator didn't bring about any consolation, either. "[Brian] Reese just kind of sat there, like he could have been anywhere," Tonya added. "He didn't show any emotions at all that I saw."

The defense was fighting an uphill battle at this trial, though Shircliff tried his best to see that Brian Reese received a fair trial. During a recess, when the jurors were out of the courtroom, he asked the judge for a mistrial because he had discovered that two jurors who had arrived at the courthouse early had seen Brian being brought into court wearing handcuffs and leg shackles. The defense feared that this would prejudice them against Brian. When his motion for a mistrial was denied, Shircliff then asked that at least the two jurors who saw Brian be removed. Judge Borges brought the two jurors in and asked them if what they saw would prejudice them against Brian Reese, and they both said no. The judge even questioned Brian, and he told the judge that, yes, he saw the two jurors looking at him. Regardless, the judge said she could find no reason to remove the jurors, and the trial continued.

Next up, the prosecution called Detective Randall Cook to the witness stand. He told the jurors about learning that Lona Bishop may possibly have been involved in the Clifford Haddix robbery and murder, and about how he had sent the narcotics detectives to her house on North Hamilton Street to bring her in for an interview. The defense attorney cross-examined Detective Cook but basically just reviewed what he had said.

The prosecution next presented a stipulation to the court. The defense had no objection to offering into evidence the police radio transmissions from the incident at 215 North Hamilton Street, along with the vehicle chase of Brian and his mother and the incident in the 800 block of North Euclid Avenue.

The prosecution then asked Detective Ryan Vanoeveren, one of the narcotics officers who had gone to pick up Lona Bishop, to take the witness stand. After being sworn in, the detective told the court about how he and the three other narcotics detectives had driven together to 215 North Hamilton Avenue at around 2:30 P.M. on July 10, 2008. He said that all four of them had been wearing their badges on chains around their necks and had their guns exposed. He went on to say that as he and Detective Chris Smith walked up toward the front door, it opened and a white male started to come out. Vanoeveren then pointed to Brian Reese in the courtroom and identified him as the man he'd seen coming out of the door that day. He said they asked about Lona Bishop and if they could speak with her, and that he seemed very nervous. The man mumbled something to them about putting his dog up and darted back into the house, locking the door.

Detective Vanoeveren told the jurors that there was a window next to the door and that he stepped over and looked through it. He said he saw two white females in the living room, and an older white male standing just inside the kitchen. Detective Vanoeveren was trying to talk to the older female through the window when he heard the detectives at the rear of the house shouting over the police radio that a man with a gun had just jumped out of a window. He and Detective Smith immediately ran in the direction the detectives in the rear said the man with the gun was heading and they saw Brian cut through some yards and then head north on Hamilton Avenue. The detectives chased after him and saw him turn west on New York Street. He was pretty far ahead of them, and they lost sight of him when he turned and ran south in the first alley west of Hamilton Avenue.

In response to the prosecutor's next question, Vanoeveren said he could see that Brian was carrying a gun in his left hand as he fled from the officers. Upon losing sight of Brian, he continued, the detectives returned to 215

North Hamilton, where they spoke with the older woman, Rosemary Bishop, Lona's mother. She seemed scared to talk about Brian with the officers, but she did finally tell them that that's who it was who ran. Lona had at first claimed that the person who fled the house was a man she was dating by the name of Steven Fillipo.

On cross-examination, defense attorney Laura Pitts asked Detective Vanoeveren if Brian Reese had ever pointed the gun at him. He answered no, he hadn't.

Following Detective Vanoeveren, Detective Chris Smith stepped up to testify. Upon being sworn in, he told the jurors about how, after hearing the radio broadcast from the officers at the rear of the house, he had seen Brian Reese cut through a vacant lot a few houses north of them and then run out onto Hamilton Avenue and west on New York Street. He said that by the time he and the other detectives returned to 215 North Hamilton, the older white male had fled the scene. He repeated the story about Lona at first claiming that the man who ran from the police was Steven Fillipo.

Laura Pitts again handled the cross-examination, and once more she asked if Brian Reese had ever pointed the gun at him. Detective Smith said no, he hadn't.

After Detective Smith finished his testimony the court broke for lunch. Before the jury returned to the courtroom the defense once again objected to Jason Fishburn sitting in the courtroom, and Judge Borges once again denied the objection.

Following lunch, the first witness called by the prosecution was Lona Bishop. She took the witness stand and told the jurors that the house at 215 North Hamilton Avenue belonged to her mother. She then said that she first met Brian Reese in 2003 or 2004, and that on July 10, 2008, he was her boyfriend (though apparently not any longer). Just before the police arrived, she said, Brian and his father, Paul Reese Sr., were getting ready to go to a nearby gas station. When Brian saw the police out front, Lona went on, he slammed the door and locked it, then started shouting, "It's the Feds! It's the Feds!" By this time, she said, he was already halfway out the bedroom window.

Lona admitted that she gave the police a fake name when they asked who had just fled the house with a gun. She said she also told the police, after admitting that it had been Brian, that he would likely go to his mother's house. The prosecution then turned Lona over to the defense for questioning.

Laura Pitts once again handled the cross-examination. She first had Lona basically repeat her earlier testimony, and then asked her if she smoked crack cocaine. Lona answered that yes, she did. She said that she and Brian had smoked some crack very early in the morning of July 10, 2008. When asked how much they smoked, Lona replied a "thirty piece," meaning thirty dollars' worth of crack cocaine. Pitts thanked her and turned her back over to the prosecution for redirect examination.

Deputy prosecutor Denise Robinson asked Lona how she and Brian smoked the crack, and Lona answered in a pipe. She said that the effect of the thirty piece lasted about three to four hours. Robinson then asked Lona how Brian acted when he smoked crack cocaine.

"Hyper, very, very hyper," Lona answered. "He can't sit still. He gets fidgety, talks a lot."

"Does he get violent?" Robinson asked.

"No."

"Out of his head crazy?"

"No."

"Was Brian hyper when he got ready to leave the house to go to the gas station?"

"No, he wasn't."

Robinson then turned Lona over to the defense for recross examination. Pitts asked Lona if she had still been under the effect of the drugs she had smoked when the detectives took her down to police headquarters for questioning. She said that yes, she had still been a little affected. Ms. Pitts asked Lona if she was "tweaking" then, which Lona explained to the court meant that a person desperately needed some more drugs. Lona said that yes, she had wanted some more crack.

Once Lona Bishop left the witness stand, the prosecution next called her mother, Rosemary Bishop, to testify. She told the jurors that on the afternoon of July 10, 2008, she had been sleeping on a couch in the living room but had woken up when she heard Brian and Paul Sr. getting ready to go to the gas station. She then told the same story about Brian telling the officers he had to put his dog up, and then locking the front door and running into the bedroom. Rosemary said she eventually let the police officers inside and at first didn't tell the police it had been Brian Reese who fled, but finally did. She said

Dawn Marie Stuard was thirteen years old when she was murdered on March 16, 1986. *(Courtesy of Ted Stuard)*

Uniformed police officers and detectives at the site on East 23rd Street where Dawn Marie Stuard's body was found on March 17, 1986.   (© The Indianapolis Star)

Police chaplain (wearing the hat), stands with Dawn's parents, Ted and Sandy Stuard, at the crime scene on East 23rd Street.
(© The Indianapolis Star)

The Reese home on North Bosart Street still looks much as it did in 1986. *(Robert L. Snow)*

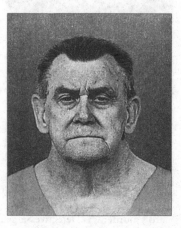

Detectives arrested Paul Reese Sr. (shown here in a 2011 mugshot) in 1986 for Dawn Marie Stuard's murder, but later released him for lack of evidence. *(Indianapolis Metropolitan Police Department)*

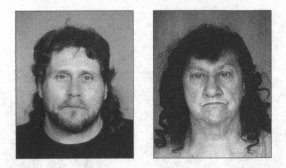

Left: Paul Reese Jr. (shown here in a 2013 mugshot) was arrested with his father in 1986 for Dawn Marie Stuard's murder, but later released for lack of evidence. *Right:* Barbara Reese (shown here in a 2012 mugshot) was arrested in 2008 for trying to help her son, Brian, escape from the police.

(Indianapolis Metropolitan Police Department)

Dawn Marie Stuard's murder was Detective Sergeant Roy West's first case as a homicide detective, and he never gave up in his determination to solve it.

(Indianapolis Metropolitan Police Department)

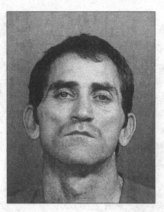

The police suspected Brian Reese of having been involved in multiple crimes, including several murders.

(Indianapolis Metropolitan Police Department)

Lona Bishop's house on North Hamilton Avenue, where police detectives first encountered Brian Reese on July 10, 2008.

(Robert L. Snow)

The crime scene on North Euclid Avenue, where Officer Jason Fishburn was shot and critically injured during his chase of Brian Reese on July 10, 2008.   *(Robert L. Snow)*

Officer Jason Fishburn and his wife, Tonya, who married in 2002.
                                        (Courtesy of Dennis Fishburn)

Officer Jason Fishburn came from a close-knit law enforcement
family. *(Courtesy of Dennis Fishburn)*

Officer Jason Fishburn and his wife, Tonya, who worked for the
county crime lab. *(Courtesy of Dennis Fishburn)*

Ted Stuard never doubted that the Reese family was involved in the murder of his daughter. Over two decades later, he and his second wife, Linda Stuard, both played key roles in getting Dawn's murder case reopened. *(Courtesy of Ted and Linda Stuard)*

Left: Detective Mark Albert of the Indianapolis Metropolitan Police Department Cold Case Squad reopened the Dawn Marie Stuard murder case in 2011, with assistance from retired detective Roy West. *(Courtesy of Mark Albert)*

Right: Deputy prosecutor Denise Robinson prosecuted both the Officer Jason Fishburn shooting case and the Dawn Marie Stuard murder case. *(Courtesy of Denise A. Robinson)*

she had been scared. The prosecutor thanked her and turned her over to the defense for cross-examination.

Rosemary told the defense attorney that she hadn't withheld from the police the name of the man who had run from them because she was scared of Brian, but because she was scared of Paul Reese Sr. The defense attorney asked Rosemary if she was aware of Brian and Lona's drug usage, and she said yes, she was. The defense attorney next asked her how her daughter Lona acted after smoking crack.

"She gets very angry," Rosemary responded. "She goes off on everything."

"Do you think Lona was under the effect of drugs when she went down to the police station to talk to the detectives?"

"No."

The defense attorney said she had no more questions. The prosecution had no redirect questions, so the judge told the prosecution to call its next witness. They called Detective Aaron Tevebaugh to the witness stand.

Detective Tevebaugh told the same story about going to the house on North Hamilton Street and the foot chase. Then he told the jurors that, after learning the identity of the two men at the house on North Hamilton, he went back to his office to get pictures of Brian and Paul Sr. He said that during this time they received information that Paul Sr. might have headed for his father's house at 1210 East Washington Street, so he set up surveillance there in case Brian also showed up. However, Tevebaugh said, he was pulled off this surveillance and told to instead assist with the surveillance of Brian's mother on Bosart Street.

Next, Detective Tevebaugh told the court that he heard the chase and the shots fired report on the police radio as he was headed to assist in the surveillance. He stopped his car at East 10th and North Linwood and then ran over to the 800 block of North Euclid, but by the time he arrived, the situation was over. He said that he saw Brian Reese lying handcuffed on the ground and that he had soot marks on his arms.

During cross-examination, Pitts asked Detective Tevebaugh if Brian ever pointed the gun at him. He answered no, he hadn't. With no redirect questions from the prosecution, the judge excused the detective from the stand.

The prosecution next called Detective Chad Osborne to testify. After being sworn in, he told the court that he drove the Chevrolet TrailBlazer that day, and then the same story about the house on North Hamilton. He said that he saw Brian Reese run across two lots north of the house on North Hamilton, then out and north on Hamilton, and finally west on New York Street. He also saw the gun in Brian's hand as he ran.

Following the incident on North Hamilton, Osborne said he went with an Officer Jamie Guilfoy to the 1400 block of North Bosart Street to set up surveillance on Brian's mother. He said he saw a white minivan stop in front of the Reese house but then continue on. The minivan returned a few minutes later, and Barbara Reese exited the minivan with a bag of groceries and went inside. She came back out a few minutes later and got back into the white minivan and drove away. He did not follow her; he said he was told to stay where he was and continue the surveillance. He told the court that he later heard the police radio traffic about Detective Jeff Wood saying he had seen the white minivan pick up Brian Reese, about the attempt to stop the minivan, the chase, and the shots fired report on North Euclid. At that point, Osborne said, he went over to the crime scene on North Euclid, but that there were already lots of officers on the scene tending to Jason Fishburn, so he helped move cars out of the way to make a clear path so that the ambulance could get through. He said that he recognized the man under arrest there on North Euclid as the same one they had chased on North Hamilton, although the man had different clothes on, and his face and arms were covered with soot.

The defense again asked on cross-examination if Brian Reese had ever pointed the gun he carried at him. Detective Osborne answered no, he hadn't. The judge excused him.

The prosecution followed Detective Osborne's testimony by calling Detective Tim Day to the witness stand. Detective Day said that on July 10, 2008, he worked for the Violent Crimes Unit of the Indianapolis Metropolitan Police Department. He told the jurors that he went with Detective Jeff Wood and several other officers to set up surveillance on Barbara Reese. He said that he parked down the street from the house while Detective Wood sat closer. He then told the same story about the white minivan stopping at the house and then picking up Brian at the church. He said he pulled away and joined Detective Wood as he tried to stop the van. Detective Day added that at 10th and Linwood, several marked police cars with their flashing lights and sirens turned on converged on the intersection. The van paused briefly and then swerved around the police cars and headed south. Barbara stopped the van for a second in the 900 block of North Linwood but then took off again. When the white minivan pulled into the parking lot of the Linwood Square Shopping Center, police cars came from all directions and blocked the vehicle's path. Barbara stopped and Brian leaped out and ran.

Prosecutor Denise Robinson then asked Detective Day, "Did you see what the driver of the [van] was doing at this time?"

"Yeah, she exited the vehicle and tried to run toward the street," he answered.

"She didn't get very far?"

"No, ma'am."

Detective Day continued by saying that he joined in the foot chase of Brian Reese and that all of them were yelling, "Stop! Police!" He said he lost sight of Brian due to a privacy fence just beyond the guardrail. When he heard the first gunshots, he raced around the privacy fence and a few seconds later he saw the officers shoot Brian Reese. He then pointed out for the court the man he'd seen shot that day by pointing to the defendant Brian Reese.

Day went on to say that he spotted a revolver on the ground near Brian and then heard the other officers yelling, "Where's Fish? Where's Fish? He's not answering his radio!" Detective Day said that he ran over with the other officers to where Fishburn lay on the ground, and that he saw Fishburn's Taser on the ground nearby. Prosecutor Denise Robinson thanked him and then turned him over to the defense.

Defense attorney David Shircliff handled the cross-examination. He went over Detective Day's story of the surveillance and pursuit of Barbara's minivan, then asked him to describe the scene in front of the Kroger's store in Linwood Square. Detective Day told the jurors how Brian had jumped out of the minivan and actually ran into the right rear of a police vehicle that had stopped in front of him. He bounced off, though, and continued to run. The detective then told again about the foot chase. Shircliff asked Detective Day if he had personally seen the revolver in Brian's hand. He answered no, he hadn't.

"Was Brian Reese facedown on the ground when you arrived?" Shircliff asked Day.

"No, he was on his side."

Shircliff then went over the story of Day and the other officers finding Fishburn, and finished by asking, "You never saw Brian Reese brandish a weapon? Correct?"

"Correct."

The defense then turned Detective Day back over to the prosecution for redirect. Robinson asked him, "Did you see any weapons in Fishburn's hands, either?"

"No, ma'am," Day replied.

The prosecution next called Donna Pike to testify. After she took the witness stand and was sworn in, she told the court that on July 10, 2008, she was headed with her daughter and two grandchildren to the Kroger's store in the Linwood Square Shopping Center. She and her family had cut through the apartment area just south of the shopping center when suddenly a man ran past them really fast with two people chasing him. She thought it likely that he was a shoplifter. The three people all ran past the guardrail and privacy fence, and a few moments later she heard gunshots. That was the extent of her testimony, so the prosecution gave her over to the defense for cross-examination.

Shircliff went over again what she had seen, and asked if the police officers chasing the man had their guns out.

"No," she answered.

"Did you see anything in the hands of the person being chased?"

"No."

Donna Pike then said that she definitely heard more than two gunshots. Shircliff asked if she saw anything after the men went around the privacy fence, and she answered no, she hadn't. With no more questions from either side, the judge excused her.

The prosecution followed that witness's testimony by calling another one to the witness stand. After being sworn in, Terri Combs told the jurors that on July 10, 2008, she lived in the 800 block of North Euclid Avenue and had been sitting out on her porch.

"I was sitting there and I heard a lot of ruckus," she

told the court. "I looked to my left and I could see a person running and an officer chasing him saying, 'Halt! Police!' He leaps over the guardrail, and the cop runs right behind him over the guardrail, then he comes up to the left side of the double where I live. As soon as he got to the side of my house, I jumped up and I ran into the house and locked the door." The police officer, she told the court, carried what looked like a gun in his right hand.

Following this, she said, she crawled toward her kitchen and heard gunshots. She then peeked out of her kitchen window and saw the officers chasing Brian Reese. She ran down to her basement.

"I looked out my basement door and right there lying at my back door was Officer Fishburn. The officers that were working on him kept saying, 'Fish, stay with us! Fish, stay with us!'"

She said that as the officers were working on Fishburn, she called 911. When asked why she had called when she saw that the police were already there, she said, "It was just instinct." She then listened to a recording of her 911 call and verified it. The prosecutor thanked her and allowed the defense to start their cross-examination.

Defense attorney David Shircliff asked Terri Combs if there was a gap in the privacy fence on July 10, 2008, and she said yes, there was. He then went over her earlier story of what she had seen and done, and asked if the running man had had a gun out. She said no, she didn't see one. She then identified Brian Reese as the man she saw being chased, and said that Officer Fishburn had been about fifteen feet behind him.

"You never saw anyone fire a weapon? Correct?" Shircliff asked her.

"No, I didn't."

Shircliff then handed the witness back to the prosecution for redirect. Denise Robinson showed Terri Combs a Taser and asked her if that could have been what she saw in Fishburn's hand. The witness said that the Taser sure looked like a gun. Shircliff objected and the judge sustained the objection. The prosecution thanked Terri Combs and the judge excused her.

Next up, the prosecution called Detective John Howard to the witness stand. After being sworn in, he told the court that on July 10, 2008, he, too, had worked for the Violent Crimes Unit of the Indianapolis Metropolitan Police Department (as had detectives Jeff Wood and Tim Day). On that day, he said, he received an assignment to conduct surveillance on a house at 1428 North Bosart Street. He told the court that his car had small police badges on the front quarter panels, so he couldn't get right up on the house without being noticed.

He said he'd tried to help tail the white minivan Barbara Reese drove, and spoke about how it had stopped in front of the Kroger's store and a man had jumped out of it and ran. Detective Howard then identified Brian Reese as the man he'd seen fleeing from the minivan. He also said he saw Brian Reese bounce off of a police car that stopped directly in front of him, and then run around the back of the car and flee south. Howard said he jumped out of his own car and joined the foot pursuit, and that when he was about ten feet from the guardrail, he heard several gunshots. As he continued running, he said he slipped and fell, and the other officers ran past him. When he got up he heard several more gunshots. He then looked around the privacy fence and saw several officers approaching Brian Reese, who lay on the ground.

Detective Howard told the jurors that he raced over to the fallen Reese and handcuffed him. He said he could see a growing bloodstain on Reese's left shoulder and called on his radio for medical assistance for him. He also noticed a long-barreled revolver lying on the ground near Reese. He added that he stayed and guarded Brian Reese while the other officers went in search of the missing Officer Jason Fishburn.

Defense attorney David Shircliff, conducting the cross-examination, went over Detective Howard's testimony about the pursuit and stopping of the white minivan. Then he asked, "Did you see a weapon in Brian Reese's hand while he was in the van?"

"No, sir," Howard answered.

"Did you see a weapon in Brian Reese's hand when he jumped out of the van?"

"No, sir."

"Did you see any of the exchanges between Brian Reese and the other officers?"

"No, sir."

Shircliff said that this concluded his cross-examination, and the prosecution told the judge that they had no redirect.

Reserve Sergeant Jim Dora next took the witness stand for the prosecution. After being sworn in, he told the court that he had been an Indianapolis Metropolitan Police Department reserve officer for eighteen years and that on July 10, 2008, he had been working the 7:00 P.M. to 3:00 A.M. shift. He said that on that date, he was meeting with another reserve officer at the Linwood Square Shopping Center. They were going to coordinate their patrol that night of a high-crime area around East 42nd Street and North Mitthoeffer Road. Dora said that they heard the call for help in stopping a white minivan over the police radio, and they went to assist. He helped chase the white minivan into the shopping center and witnessed Brian Reese jump from the van and flee. Dora said that he then left his vehicle and ran south down the row of apartments east of the route Brian used, in case he came that way.

When he reached the end of the apartments, Dora said, he saw the officers jumping over the guardrail and heading south on North Euclid Avenue. He raced down there, and when he came around the privacy fence and onto Euclid Avenue he heard shots but didn't see who fired them. Dora then saw Brian Reese run out from between some houses and heard more gunshots. He said he didn't see who fired their guns or if Brian Reese had a gun. At the moment, he'd been looking for cover because he knew he was exposed. Dora told the jurors that he did see the long-barreled revolver lying on the ground close to Brian. He then identified Brian Reese as the man they were chasing that day. The prosecutor thanked him and told the defense that Sergeant Dora was available for cross-examination.

Defense attorney David Shircliff went over Sergeant Dora's story about the foot chase and then asked him the same questions he had asked Detective Howard about seeing a gun in Brian's hand. Sergeant Dora, like Detective Howard, replied no to all of these questions.

Judge Borges, at the beginning of the trial, when she gave the jurors their initial instructions, told them that if they had any questions of the witnesses they were to write them down and give them to the bailiff. The judge would then read the questions, and if she felt they were proper she would ask them of the witness. One of the jurors wanted to know if Sergeant Dora heard the officers say anything to Brian Reese. He answered no, he didn't. Another juror asked where Brian Reese was lying specifically, and Sergeant Dora showed them on a diagram of the crime scene. Finally, another juror asked Sergeant Dora if he ever saw a gun in Brian's hand. He answered no. These questions finished, the judge excused the sergeant.

Deputy prosecutor Denise Robinson next asked Officer Jerry Piland to take the witness stand. Upon being sworn in, Piland told the jurors that on July 10, 2008, he worked as a uniformed officer on the East District. He said that just before Detective Wood had called for assistance in stopping the white minivan, he and Fishburn had been on a disturbance run involving a fight between a mother and daughter who lived in the Linwood Square Apartments. As they were leaving the run, they heard Detective Wood calling for assistance over his radio.

Piland said that as he and Fishburn went to East 10th

Street and North Linwood Avenue they saw the white minivan heading south on Linwood toward them. They turned on their emergency lights and sirens, but the minivan swerved around them and continued south on Linwood Avenue. He said the van accelerated and tried to get away from them, then suddenly made a move as though it was going to turn into the first entrance to the shopping center, but instead continued on and turned into the second entrance. The van stopped suddenly in front of the Kroger's store and then Brian Reese jumped out and ran.

"I slammed on the brakes," Piland told the court, "which caused him [Reese], as he tried to run behind my car, to run into my rear quarter panel. He rolled over the trunk and continued running towards the courtyard of the apartment complex."

Piland continued his story by describing how he jumped out of his car and ran after Brian while giving a clothing description and direction of travel over the police radio. He said that he saw Fishburn and Brian just ahead of him, and also saw Fishburn pull out his Taser, but didn't see it have any noticeable effect on Brian. He added that he was about fifteen to twenty yards behind the two of them.

Rather than running down Euclid Avenue, Piland said, he ran over to the alley east of Euclid in order to try to cut Brian off. He said he didn't make it to the alley, though, because he heard gunshots. He immediately reported this on his police radio and took cover behind a car. A few seconds later, Piland added, he heard officers yelling for someone to get down and stay down. He then saw the officers running up to Brian Reese, and he ran over and helped Detective Howard secure him.

"I then started looking around," Piland told the jurors, "and I noticed that Jason wasn't there, and I couldn't figure out why because he was right on the suspect's heels as they started to run between those two houses."

He then told about the officers calling for Fishburn and trying to contact him on the radio. They then checked between the two houses and found him. Piland said that Fishburn had vomit on his face and that they wiped it off.

"We ripped open his shirt and I pulled his vest up and I could see a big nasty swollen area just above his belly button," Piland told the jurors. "I said, 'Jason, you're good. You're good. Your vest took the shot. You're going to be okay.' At about this time though is when he turned his head and I could see that he had a hole behind his ear that was bleeding pretty badly."

Once he finished his story, Robinson thanked him and sat down.

Defense attorney David Shircliff went over Officer Piland's story of the foot chase and then asked the same questions about whether he ever saw a gun in Brian's hand. Piland answered no to all of these questions.

Judge Borges then read several questions the jurors had of Officer Piland, starting with, "Is it standard to carry a Taser?"

"Yes, the majority of officers carry one."

The judge then allowed Piland to show the jury his own Taser.

"When you removed Officer Fishburn's gun belt, where was his gun?" another juror wanted to know.

"It was lying to his left side on the ground. His Taser was also out of its holster and lying towards his feet."

The judge then asked, because of a juror's question, if Officer Piland would unholster and display his Glock semiautomatic pistol and his Taser so that the jury could see if they looked alike or different. Once Officer Piland had done this, the judge thanked him and told him that he could step down.

Detective Sergeant Leslie VanBuskirk next took the witness stand for the prosecution. She told the court that she was a homicide unit supervisor and also a member of the Critical Incident Response Team (CIRT). She said that part of her responsibilities as a member of CIRT was to respond to officer-involved shootings, so she went to Wishard Memorial Hospital right after hearing about the Fishburn/Reese shooting on Euclid Avenue. She arrived there at 7:23 P.M., shortly before both Officer Jason Fishburn and Brian Reese. VanBuskirk said that after talking with Sergeant Snyder and Officer Piland, she took possession of Fishburn's clothing and then transported it back to the Homicide Office for the Crime Lab to examine.

Deputy prosecutor Denise Robinson then had Detective Sergeant VanBuskirk show the jury the clothing that had been cut off of Fishburn. It was in large, clear evidence bags.

Defense attorney David Shircliff had no cross-examination but did ask the judge to remove the jury so that he could make a motion.

When the jury had left the courtroom, Shircliff made a motion that he wanted to go on record as objecting anytime the term "homicide" or "homicide detective" was used. According to Indiana law, the prosecution cannot, with individuals on trial for a specific crime, bring up any other crimes the defendant is suspected of, charged with, or convicted of. Shircliff feared that it would prejudice the jury if they knew Brian Reese was a suspect in other homicides. The judge noted the motion.

The prosecution, once the jury had returned to the courtroom, brought a new witness to the stand. Once sworn in, Lisa Liebig told the court that she worked at the Marion County Crime Lab as a crime scene specialist. She established her credentials and talked for a few minutes about her training and experience, then she told the jurors how she'd responded to a call to process the crime scene for the Fishburn/Reese shooting at 7:50 P.M. on July 10, 2008. She said she started at the Kroger's store and worked her way to the 800 block of Euclid Avenue, making diagrams, taking photos, and searching for evidence.

"Did you record the vehicle identification number of the minivan the police chased?" Ms. Robinson asked her.

"Yes, it was registered to a Barbara Reese of 1428 North Bosart Street."

The prosecution then had her run through a set of photographs of the crime scene on an overhead projector, showing the jurors the general area and specifically where she had recovered evidence, such as shell casings, drops of blood, Officer Fishburn's Taser, his .40 caliber Glock semiautomatic pistol, and the long-barreled .38 caliber Smith & Wesson revolver. The prosecution then had Liebig hold up the front panel of Fishburn's bulletproof vest and show the jury where she had removed a .38 caliber bullet from it.

Following this, the crime scene specialist testified that when she examined the .38 caliber revolver, she found that it had five spent casings and one live bullet in the cylinder. She then showed the jurors photos of the Glocks belonging to Officers Wood and Scott, the two officers who had shot Brian Reese. The magazine of Scott's gun, she said, had nine live rounds in it, and she found one live round in the firing chamber, meaning that he had fired at least five rounds. The magazine of Wood's gun had fourteen live rounds in it, and she also found one live round in the firing chamber, meaning that he had fired only one round.

Moving on to another subject, Robinson asked if Liebig found any fingerprints on the evidence she recovered. She said no, she didn't, but that she did take DNA swabs from the evidence. She then spoke in great detail about how she'd taken the swabs for DNA from the .38 caliber revolver recovered at the crime scene. She said she took swabs from the grip, the trigger, the hammer, the muzzle, and from the one live round in the cylinder. She also noted that she'd found six live .38 caliber rounds in a holster that Brian Reese had allegedly dropped at the crime scene, but again no fingerprints. Overall, she told the jurors, she spent fourteen hours at the crime scene. The prosecution thanked her and then handed her over to the defense for cross-examination.

After walking her through her credentials and what she did that day at the crime scene, defense attorney Jeffrey Neel asked, "Did you find any bullet holes near where Officer Fishburn had been shot?"

"No, I didn't," Liebig answered.

"Did you use a metal detector that night at the crime scene?"

"No, I didn't."

Neel then attempted to get Liebig to acknowledge that the crime scene was confused and cluttered. She said that debris from where medical personnel had worked on an injured subject always cluttered a crime scene. He then questioned whether Liebig had done a thorough job at the crime scene, since, he pointed out, the wires from the Taser round that Officer Jason Fishburn had fired at Brian Reese weren't found until several days later. Liebig simply responded that she had done as thorough a job as possible under the circumstances. Neel then finished his cross-examination by asking her again if she had found any bullet holes around where Officer Fishburn had been shot, and she again said she hadn't.

On redirect examination, the prosecution asked, "Is it uncommon for all of the medical debris to be at a crime scene?"

"No, it isn't," Liebig responded.

"And you didn't find any bullet holes around where Jason had been shot?"

"No."

Lisa Liebig finished her redirect testimony by telling the jury that she did return with a metal detector to the crime scene in March 2009. Rather than excusing the crime scene specialist at this point, however, the judge said that the jurors had some questions.

"How many rounds does a .40 caliber Glock carry?" the judge read.

"It depends on the model of the Glock."

"Was Fishburn's Taser fired?"

"The end cap was off of it," Liebig responded, "but I don't know if it was fired. Tasers are not my specialty."

With the juror questions finished, the judge excused Liebig and she left the witness stand.

The prosecution next brought Detective Michael Bain to the witness stand. Bain told the jurors that he worked in the Dangerous Drugs Section of the Indianapolis Metropolitan Police Department, and before that he had worked for three years as a homicide detective. He said that he had been in the Homicide Office when the call came out for Homicide to go to the 800 block of North Euclid. The run went to Detective Sergeant Breedlove, but he went along to assist him. He said that they worked at the crime scene until around 10:30 P.M.

In addition to being a detective, Bain told the court, he was also a firearms expert, so deputy prosecutor Denise Robinson followed up on the jury questions and asked him about the number of bullets that various models of Glock can carry. Bain said that the Indianapolis Metropolitan Police Department issued two models of

Glock. The Model 23 can carry thirteen rounds in the magazine and one in the firing chamber, while the Model 22 can carry fifteen rounds in the magazine and one in the firing chamber. (The prosecution wanted this testimony because it felt that earlier the defense was trying to make an issue of there being fourteen rounds in Detective Wood's gun, even though he said he had fired at Brian Reese.) Detective Bain finished his testimony by telling the jury that the Glocks the police department used don't have an external safety.

After a short cross-examination that didn't bring up any new information, the judge excused him.

The prosecution next had Mike Kouns walk up and take a seat in the witness chair. After Kouns was sworn in, he told the jury that he was a crime scene specialist and technical team leader for the Marion County Crime Lab. He also responded to the crime scene on North Euclid. The prosecution then asked him many of the same questions it had asked his colleague Lisa Liebig and received similar answers.

The defense, upon cross-examination, asked Kouns, "Did you use a metal detector that night at the crime scene?"

"No, we didn't," he responded.

"Was this Ms. Liebig's first major crime scene?"

"Yes, it was."

Mike Kouns then went on to explain that that was why he went along to the crime scene, to be certain that Lisa Liebig did everything properly. He next told the court that the reason they went back later with the metal detector was because more shots had been fired than bullet casings recovered.

The defense finished the cross-examination by asking, "Did you find any bullet holes in the houses where Officer Fishburn had been shot?"

"No, we didn't."

Again, the judge asked the witness to remain while she read some questions the jurors had.

"Why wasn't a metal detector used where Officer Fishburn was?"

"There was too much junk lying around for it to be useful," Mr. Kouns said.

"Is it common to use a metal detector?"

"Not always. It depends on the location. And usually shell casings are visible on the ground."

With these questions answered, the judge excused the witness.

The prosecution then called Lisa Prater to the witness stand, another crime scene specialist for the Marion County Crime Lab. She told the jurors that she hadn't been at the original crime scene on July 10, 2008, but that she had been called to do a follow-up search of the crime scene on July 14, 2008. She said she was the one who recovered the Taser pins from Officer Fishburn's Taser near the guardrail. She also recovered a .40 caliber casing close to where Officer Fishburn had been lying. Robinson thanked her and then turned the witness over to the defense for cross-examination.

"Did a detective call you to the crime scene on July 14th?" the defense asked.

"Yes, Detective Howard had found the items and wanted me to collect them."

"Did you use a metal detector on July 14th? The items you recovered, after all, were metal."

"No, I didn't."

When the defense finished, the judge then read Lisa Prater a question one of the jurors had.

"Is it common to go back to a crime scene to look for more evidence?"

"Yes, it is."

The judge excused the crime scene specialist, and the prosecution then called Detective Jeff Wood to the witness stand. He said that he worked for the Violent Crimes Unit of the Indianapolis Metropolitan Police Department, and that on July 10, 2008, he received a call from Detective John Howard to assist in surveillance at 1428 North Bosart Street. He then went through the same story about seeing Barbara Reese in the white minivan and chasing it, and then about witnessing Brian Reese jumping out of the minivan and fleeing. He said he joined in the foot pursuit and heard gunfire come from the Euclid Street area. He ran into that area.

"As I was moving southwesterly through the yards," he told the jurors, "Brian Reese appeared from between the houses running eastbound. He was carrying a gun in his left hand. He then abruptly pivoted on his left foot, and instead of running east he turned and began to run back southward. The handgun that he had in his left hand came up and he started to raise it toward me. I fired my weapon."

He said that Reese continued to run around the side of a nearby house, but because he had been shot he fell down. Detective Wood then ran over and covered him as Detective Howard put handcuffs on him.

The prosecution thanked him and turned Detective Wood over to the defense.

"You saw a gun in Brian Reese's left hand?" defense attorney David Shircliff asked.

"Yes."

"Did he raise the gun towards you?"

"Yes, he did."

"Did he shoot at you?"

"No."

"At Detective Scott?"

"No."

"At any of the other officers?"

"No."

"Did Brian Reese have a gun out when he jumped out of the van?"

"No."

"Did Brian Reese have a gun out when Officer Fishburn fired his Taser?"

"No."

The judge, upon completion of the cross-examination, then read a question from one of the jurors.

"Did you know that Brian Reese had been shot when he continued to run around the house?"

"No."

Detective Steve Scott then took the witness stand after the judge had excused Detective Wood. Detective

Scott told the jurors that on July 10, 2008, he also worked for the Violent Crimes Unit. He then told the same story about the surveillance, chase, and foot pursuit. He said that when he reached the guardrail he heard gunshots and then ran onto Euclid Avenue. He saw Brian Reese come from between two houses and suddenly point his revolver at him. He fired several shots at Reese, who continued running around the side of a house. He said they chased after him and found him lying up against the house. When asked how many rounds he fired that day, he said he had ten bullets left in his gun, and he had started with fifteen.

The prosecution finished with its questioning, and the defense then asked, "Did you get shot at that day?"

"No."

"Did you see Brian Reese with a weapon during the initial foot chase?"

"No."

Detective Scott stepped down, and deputy prosecutor Mark Hollingsworth took over the questioning.

The prosecution next called Timothy Spears, who told the court that he was a forensic scientist at the Marion County Crime Lab, and that he was assigned to the firearms section. He told the court that he was qualified as an expert witness on firearms examination.

"We've heard previous testimony that a bullet was recovered from an officer's bullet-resistant vest," Hollingsworth said. "Were you able to examine that bullet in relationship to the revolver [recovered from Brian Reese]?"

"Yes. That bullet was fired from that firearm. Also,

the bullet that went into the bulletproof vest had been fired from at least six feet away because there was no powder residue."

The defense, in its cross-examination, then asked Spears about a bullet fragment found at the scene. He said he couldn't tell which gun it came from. Following this, the judge read a juror's question.

"Was the bullet that struck Officer Fishburn coming from upward, straight on, or a downward angle?"

"I really don't know," Spears answered.

Prosecutor Carl Brizzi then put Dr. Richard Rogers, the neurosurgeon who had led the team that operated on Officer Jason Fishburn at Wishard Memorial Hospital, on the stand. Dr. Rogers talked about the extent and seriousness of Fishburn's injuries, and about how most people with similar injuries typically didn't survive them. He said that gunshot wounds to the head have about a 90 percent mortality rate. He told the court that Jason Fishburn, when he saw him, had already lost two liters of blood because of the wound.

"After the surgery," he told the court, "I felt about the same as I did going into it, that I thought his chances of survival were probably on the order of 10 percent or less."

The prosecution then asked if Dr. Rogers could determine what type of bullet had caused Fishburn's injuries.

"The type of injury he sustained would be consistent with what people would think of as a standard round end bullet." This was the type of bullet found in Brian Reese's gun.

After a cross-examination that only reviewed Dr. Rogers's testimony about the type of bullet, the prosecution, upon redirect, had the doctor talk a little more about what permanent injuries Officer Fishburn had suffered.

When Dr. Rogers left the stand, this ended the day's testimony. The judge excused the jury with an admonishment not to talk about the case with anyone.

The next morning, November 6, 2009, before the bailiff brought the jury into the courtroom, both the prosecution and the defense stipulated to the taking of a buccal swab for DNA from Brian Reese, meaning that both the defense and the prosecution agreed that the swab had been taken properly and according to the prevailing guidelines for such samples.

Following this, once the jury had been seated, the prosecution called David Smith to the witness stand. Upon being sworn in, he told the court that he worked as the Serology Section Supervisor at the Marion County Crime Lab. He then testified that items from this case needing DNA testing had been sent to Strand Analytical Laboratories so that there would be no conflict of interest since Tonya Fishburn worked as a DNA specialist at the Marion County Crime Lab. He told the jurors that the items sent for DNA comparison were DNA swabs taken from the .38 caliber revolver, including from the trigger, from the hammer, from the barrel, and from the live rounds in the gun and in the holster.

The prosecution thanked the witness. However, the defense had no cross-examination.

Deputy prosecutor Denise Robinson then called

Cynthia Cale to the witness stand to be sworn in. Cale told the court that she worked as a forensic DNA analyst for Strand Analytical Laboratories, and that she did the testing on the swabs sent to their lab from the Marion County Crime Lab.

"I draw your attention to the DNA swab taken from the barrel of the Smith & Wesson revolver," Robinson said. "Can you tell the jury what your findings were?"

"I identified a DNA profile that matches the DNA profile of Brian Reese."

The defense, upon cross-examination, talked about the DNA swabs taken that didn't produce a match. Cale said that there was insufficient DNA on these to make a comparison.

Upon redirect, Robinson asked if it was true that insufficient DNA doesn't mean that it didn't come from Brian Reese. The DNA analyst said that was correct.

The judge excused Cynthia Cale, and the prosecution next called Beverlee Richardson to testify. Upon being sworn in, Richardson identified herself as an employee of the Indianapolis Metropolitan Police Department Training Academy, where she worked as a firearms instructor. She also said that she was the police department armorer, and that as such she repaired and performed maintenance on all department weapons, body armor, chemical sprays, handcuffs, and Tasers.

Following this introduction, Richardson testified that the Taser found at the crime scene on North Euclid belonged to Officer Jason Fishburn. She also told the court that Tasers have an internal computer that records every time they are fired, and that, upon examining the Taser found on North Euclid, she discovered that it had been fired on July 10, 2008. There was some discussion after this by the defense as to the accuracy of the specific time the Taser had recorded when Officer Fishburn fired it.

After this testimony, the judge read some more questions from the jurors. One of them wanted to know how a Taser worked, and Richardson explained it. Another juror wanted to know if a .38 caliber weapon is dropped, could it go off. Richardson answered it depended on the model. (Smith & Wesson revolvers, like the .38 in question at this trial, will not.)

During a short recess, while the jury was out of the courtroom, defense attorney David Shircliff again asked for a mistrial or at least the removal of the two jurors who had seen Brian Reese handcuffed and shackled. Shircliff said he felt serious concern about this because the next witness, Gary Rees, would come into the courtroom in shackles, which could easily remind and prejudice the two jurors. Judge Borges again denied the motion.

Once the jury had reentered the court, Denise Robinson of the prosecution called Gary Rees to the witness stand. He took the oath to tell the truth, and then told the court that he met Brian Reese in a holding cell for Criminal Court Room Four in downtown Indianapolis sometime in March or April 2009. (Records showed it to be March 12, 2009.) He said he was there for a pretrial hearing on an auto theft charge to which he had eventually pleaded guilty. Robinson then asked him if his plea agreement on the auto theft charge had anything to do with the testimony he was giving, and he said no, it didn't.

The prosecution then entered into evidence a letter Rees had written about what Brian Reese had allegedly said.

Rees told the jurors that when a deputy called for Reese, both of them had gotten up. This had started him and Brian talking. They found that they knew some of the same people. Brian told him that he had been in lockdown for eight months (which meant he'd had no contact with other prisoners during that time). Rees said that he must have done something pretty awful to have that happen.

"He told me," Rees said, "that he was running from the police with his hand over his shoulder pointing a gun backwards, running and he shot a cop twice. I told him he must be a pretty good shot if you're running forward with a gun pointing backwards and you're able to hit an officer twice. He gave me a smirk and said, 'That's just what I'm telling them happened.'"

The prosecution then interjected, "So the first version was shooting back over his shoulder? And the second version was?"

"The second version," Rees answered, "is that he stopped, turned around, waited for the officer to come into view, and started shooting."

Robinson again asked Rees if he was getting anything in exchange for his testimony. He said no. The prosecution then turned the witness over to the defense for cross-examination.

During the prosecution's questioning, Rees had said he asked Reese why he'd shot the officer, and Brian reportedly responded, "He's just a fucking pig. Fuck him."

This was extraordinarily damning testimony, and naturally the defense needed to neutralize it. Defense attorney Jeffrey Neel, who handled the cross-examination, tried to do this by attacking Rees's credibility, though that tactic proved difficult because Rees was receiving nothing in exchange for his testimony. When later asked why he had testified against Brian, Rees reportedly answered, "I'm a thief, not a murderer."

Defense attorney David Shircliff later told a reporter for the Indy Channel, "Anytime you have someone on the stand that says something as disrespectful as 'blanking pig' and adds a bunch of information, of course it's damaging, unless they perceive him, as I do, that he is a lying snitch. That is what he does for a living: he steals things and he lies to get benefits."

Neel tried several times to get Rees to say that he still hoped to get something in return for his testimony. However, Rees kept saying that no, he didn't.

"You like to steal things, don't you?" Neel then asked, seeming to change the direction of his questioning.

"Yes."

"You like to take things that don't belong to you?"

"Yes, sir."

"And then you lie about it, don't you?"

"No, sir," Rees insisted. "Every one of my cases has a plea agreement on it. I admit the truth and I do my time."

When asked by Neel why Brian would admit to a stranger the things Rees claimed he'd said, Rees responded he didn't know, because it sure wasn't very smart to talk about your crime if you're under arrest for murder. The defense then again asked for the jury to be removed, and, after they had been, once more asked for a mistrial. Gary Rees, the defense said, had let the jury know that Brian had been arrested for murder. The judge denied the motion.

The judge, with the jury still out of the courtroom, asked Gary Rees why he wrote the letter. "The reason I wrote the letter?" Rees responded. "He said he was going to escape and he was going to try to kill the officer and kill anyone who got in his way."

Following this, the defense asked again for a mistrial because they said that the jurors could see Mr. Rees's handcuffs and belly chain, and this would make them assume that Brian Reese was similarly incarcerated. The judge, upon denying this motion, pointed out that Mr. Rees's incarceration was blatantly apparent since he wore jail clothing and had a deputy always standing next to him, so the handcuffs and belly chain shouldn't shock the jurors.

The judge dismissed Gary Rees, and the deputy escorted him out of the court.

Once the jurors returned, the prosecutors then called Officer Sam Lasley to the witness stand. After being sworn in, Lasley told the court that he had been a member of the Indianapolis Metropolitan Police Department since 1975, a member of the SWAT team since 1978, and that he presently served as a firearms instructor.

The prosecutor then had him tell the jurors what kind of training the officers received in the use of both lethal and nonlethal force. Following this, the prosecutor asked, "On July 10, 2008, was Officer Fishburn up to date on his firearms training?"

"Yes, he was," Lasley answered.

"How many rounds does a Glock Model 22 hold?"

"Sixteen."

"Was it likely that at a chaotic crime scene like the one on Euclid Avenue that casings would be kicked around?"

"Absolutely," Lasley said. "With medical personnel and police officers going into a crime scene, shell casings can be kicked around or picked up in the tread of tires."

"Can you reload a Taser while in foot pursuit?"

"No."

Officer Lasley, at the prosecution's request, then showed the jury how a Taser worked. He next described what "tunnel vision" is and how it comes about during times of intense stress. After this, he described the bulletproof vest worn by police officers and explained to the jurors the "force continuum," meaning the type of force police officers must use in order to gain compliance, starting with verbal commands and moving all the way up to deadly force.

Following this, the prosecution turned Lasley over to the defense for cross-examination. Defense attorney Jeffrey Neel handled the questioning, and he again asked about how many rounds a Glock Model 22 carried. He also asked, "What should an officer do if a Taser doesn't work?"

"Usually drop it," Lasley answered.

The judge then read a question posed by one of the jurors. "Does clothing affect a Taser?"

"Yes, we even have winter cartridges with longer prongs," he said (i.e., in order to penetrate thicker clothing).

This ended the testimony for the day. The judge dismissed the jurors for the weekend, again with the admonishment not to talk to anyone about the case.

The next day of testimony, November 9, 2009, deputy prosecutor Denise Robinson asked Detective Sergeant Jeff Breedlove to take the witness stand. After being sworn in, he told the jurors that he was a seventeen-year veteran of the Indianapolis Metropolitan Police Department, and worked as a homicide unit supervisor. He said he became the lead detective on the Fishburn/Reese shooting, that he received the run at 7:26 P.M., and arrived at the scene at 7:36 P.M. He had the officers walk him through what had happened and then began managing the crime scene.

"I assigned certain detectives to do a canvass of the area to look for any witnesses," he responded after being asked what he did at the crime scene. "I assigned a sergeant to be with the crime lab and assist them in collecting evidence. I assigned some officers to take statements for me. I assigned a sergeant to go to the hospital, and I assigned an officer to collect the guns" (of the officers who had shot Brian Reese).

He also said he had the .38 caliber Smith & Wesson revolver recovered at the crime scene tested for DNA, and the bullet removed from Officer Fishburn's bullet-proof vest compared against the revolver. Following this, he showed the jurors a video taken of the crime scene at 800 North Euclid Avenue.

Then, to counter any claims that Brian hadn't intended to kill Fishburn when he fired the gun at him, the prosecution put into evidence several tape recordings of telephone calls that Brian had made while in jail, calls in which he talked about what had happened at the shooting site. In one of the calls, he told his girlfriend's sister, Catherine Bishop, that he and the police officer ran between a couple of houses, and "that's when I did what I did."

This was evidence directly from the lips of the accused, and from which the jurors could not only hear Brian Reese's words, but also his tone of voice, which didn't sound remorseful. Had it been secretly recorded? Had the police surreptitiously tapped the telephone Brian had used? No. There are signs posted where the inmates use the telephone that state that conversations are being recorded, and a tape recording also announces this information with each call made. One would think that inmates would be very careful about what they say on the phone, but, as demonstrated by Brian, very often they are not.

The prosecution then turned Detective Sergeant Breedlove over for cross-examination. Defense attorney David Shircliff handled the questioning. He asked several questions about Breedlove's testimony and his duties as lead detective. Then he asked, "Are you the one who decides who is a 'credible witness'?"

"Yes."

"Do you consider Gary Rees trustworthy?"

Deputy prosecutor Denise Robinson immediately objected to the question, and the judge sustained the objection.

Shircliff then asked, "To your knowledge, did Gary Rees take any notes of his conversation with Brian Reese?"

"No, other than his letter."

"Were there other people in the holding cell when Brian Reese talked to Gary Rees?"

"Yes."

The defense then presented evidence to show that there were nine other prisoners in that holding cell.

"Did you contact any of these other nine prisoners?" Shircliff asked.

"No."

Shircliff then asked about Gary Rees's claims that Brian had said his dad might take the rap for shooting the cop. Breedlove responded that this wasn't what Rees was talking about when he spoke about Brian's father taking the blame. The judge stopped the testimony and had the jurors removed from the courtroom. The judge and the attorneys then talked about several recorded jail telephone calls in which Brian had talked about having his father take the rap for the three murders "because he was sixty-some years old and didn't have anything to lose." The defense, of course, didn't want this information to come out, because a jury is not supposed to hear about any other crimes a defendant may be involved in.

After the jury returned, Shircliff moved on to another subject, trying to find holes in Gary Rees's story because Rees had claimed that Brian told him that the first shot spun the officer around and the second shot struck the officer in the back of the head. (Actually, Fishburn had been shot with his head facing forward.) However, he didn't have much luck getting Breedlove to concede anything. Finally, Shircliff asked Detective Sergeant Breedlove if Officers Scott and Wood had had their weapons taken away because they'd been involved in the shooting of Brian Reese. After Breedlove answered yes, the defense attorney sat down.

Following Breedlove's testimony, deputy prosecutor Denise Robinson stood up and said that the State rested its case.

Now it was the defense's turn. Once the prosecution had rested its case, the defense had to begin its portion of the trial. They hoped to be able to present evidence that would mitigate the shooting. The defense wanted the jury to see the shooting as tragic, but unintentional. Shircliff and his team weren't going to attempt to convince the jury that Brian was totally innocent, but rather that he had made a terrible mistake that day by shooting in the direction of Officer Fishburn. They wanted the jury to believe that Brian had never intended the consequences of what had happened.

They had a huge task in front of them.

TEN

The first witness called to testify by the defense on November 9, 2009, would be Officer Brian Mack. He told the court that he worked for the Indianapolis Metropolitan Police Department, and that in July 2008 he worked on the same shift and district as Officer Fishburn.

"Did you lose your badge that night on Euclid Avenue?" the defense asked.

"Yes."

"Was it returned to you by the defense attorney?"

"Yes."

"Do you know how many rounds Officer Fishburn carried in his Glock Model 22?"

"Sixteen."

The defense then turned Officer Mack over to Mark Hollingsworth of the prosecution for cross-examination.

"Do you know how many rounds Fishburn carried in his Glock Model 22 on July 10, 2008?"

Officer Mack answered no, not positively, and then went on to explain that there were pluses and minuses to carrying sixteen rounds as compared to fifteen in a Model 22 (carrying sixteen will sometimes weaken the spring in the magazine), and that he and Fishburn had talked about it, and Fishburn said he felt better with sixteen.

When Hollingsworth finished, the judge excused Officer Mack, and the defense next called Dan Bailey to the witness stand. After being sworn in, Mr. Bailey told the court that he worked as a paralegal for the Public Defender's Office. He told the court that he had been sent to the 800 block of North Euclid Avenue as an investigator for the Public Defender's Office. He said he used a metal detector but didn't find anything he would consider as evidence, only the police officer's lost badge. He then talked about the crime scene and how he had been there at least a half dozen times.

"Did you find any bullet casings or bullet strikes not already found?" the defense asked him.

"No."

The defense then turned him over to the prosecution for cross-examination, but the prosecution said it had no questions. The judge, however, told Mr. Bailey that the jury did have some questions.

"What area did you use the metal detector on?" one of the jurors had wanted to know.

"The area where Jason had been and the surrounding area."

"Do you have any professional training in the use of metal detectors?"

"No."

"Had you ever used a metal detector before?"

"No."

Following these jury questions, the defense then asked to put into evidence a video taken in October 2009 of the 800 block of North Euclid Avenue. The State had no objection.

After Mr. Bailey stepped down from the witness box, the defense next called Detective Sergeant Jeff Breedlove to testify. The defense showed him a video of the 800 block of North Euclid Avenue and asked him to tell the court the significance of a piece of white tape that had been placed on a fence.

"It was where a shell casing had been located," Breedlove answered.

The defense thanked him, and the judge, upon seeing that the prosecution had no cross-examination, told the defense to present its next witness.

The defense called Brian Reese to the witness stand.

Of course, it is always a gamble for a defense attorney to put a defendant on the stand—whatever benefits may come for the defense, the prosecution can do untold damage during cross-examination. However, Shircliff apparently felt that it was worth the risk in order for the jury to hear Brian's side of the story. After all, they'd already heard the prosecution's side, and if they went into the jury room with only that information, the results could easily be disastrous.

After the bailiff swore Brian in, Shircliff asked him, "Mr. Reese, Brian, we've already heard that the State is saying that you intentionally tried to kill Jason Fishburn. Is that true?"

"Yes."

"You—"

"I heard that," Brian added quickly.

"Did you intentionally try to kill Jason Fishburn?" Shircliff asked.

"No."

"Prior to or on the day of July 10, 2008, did you use any crack cocaine?"

"Yes."

"Can you tell the jury how much you think you used?"

"A lot, a couple of eight balls" (i.e., about 3.5 grams).

"Who were you smoking crack with?"

"With my girlfriend and my dad."

Brian then told the court that he had smoked crack all of July 9, 2008, through the night, and the next morning. He said his dad left for a bit but returned at about 9:00 or 10:00 A.M., and brought some more crack cocaine.

The defense then asked, "Would you say at that point in time you were or weren't addicted to crack cocaine?"

"I was addicted. I'd been smoking it for like nine years."

Brian then told the court that he, his dad, and his girlfriend, Lona, had smoked all the crack his dad had brought, and after this he and his dad were getting ready to go to a local gas station. He then talked about step-ping out the door, seeing the police officers, running back into the house, and jumping out the window. When the defense asked why he had run, he said that there was a warrant out on him for a theft and forgery charge that he hadn't shown up to court for. He then went on to tell the jurors about fleeing from the police and how every-where he ran he saw officers, and how he finally hid in a burned-out, abandoned house for several hours.

"Why do you think they were still chasing you at that point?" Shircliff asked.

"Because I was running around with a gun in my hand."

Following this, Brian explained how he'd gotten a trash bag and put some cans and junk in it, changed clothes, rubbed soot all over himself, and then walked out of the neighborhood disguised as a homeless person. He said that a man in an SUV pulled up and gave him $5.00, and said, "Looks like you could use this."

Once out of the neighborhood, Brian said, he went to the house of a man named Billy Joe, who was a cousin of his girlfriend. He had Billy Joe call Lona's house to see what was going on. After this, Brian had Billy Joe drive him back over to the area of 215 North Hamilton so that he could see what was going on. While they were there, Billy Joe told him that the cops were coming, so Brian said he jumped out of Billy Joe's truck and hid. Billy Joe took off. Brian said he then got the revolver back from where he had hidden it in a trash can and walked back to Billy Joe's house, but he wasn't there. Brian then bought

$10.00 worth of crack from a dealer nearby and started walking toward his mom's house on Bosart Street. After a few blocks, he stopped at a variety store, used the telephone, and called his mother and asked her to come pick him up. When she did, he told her he wanted to go to his brother's house, but his mom said she had to take some groceries home first, so she dropped him off at Little Flower Catholic Church while she went home.

When the defense attorney asked why she had dropped him off there, Brian said, "She lives with her boyfriend and none of us kids get along with him, and it starts a lot of problems with my mom and him and us, so I don't go over there really. I stay away when he's there."

Brian then told the court about the police trying to stop them after his mom picked him up in the van. He also told about jumping out of the van and running and how he saw a police officer right behind him. Brian said he heard the Taser make a crackling sound behind him and claimed that when he ran between the houses on Euclid Avenue he heard someone shoot at him.

"And what did you do then?" Shircliff asked.

"About middle way between the two houses I shot three times over my shoulder."

"And when you shot three times, did you look back?"

"No."

"Do you know if you hit anybody?"

"No."

Brian then claimed that he ran back out onto Euclid Avenue but never pointed his gun at anyone. He next told about being shot and falling down next to the house.

When Brian finished his story, the defense then turned him over to the prosecution for cross-examination.

"I was sitting there shaking my head, thinking I couldn't believe they expect the jury to believe this garbage," said Jason's father, Dennis Fishburn. "Reese took the stand and said he wasn't trying to shoot a police officer when he was running, he just shot over his shoulder without looking back. I wondered why he hadn't hurt his eardrum." Dennis also wasn't impressed with Brian's lack of emotion during the trial. "Reese was real nonchalant during the trial, like nothing serious was happening. Just kept a straight face most of the time. I never saw much change in his facial expression."

Marion County prosecutor Carl Brizzi had hoped that Shircliff would put Brian on the stand. "We would welcome the opportunity to chat with Brian Reese," he told the news media.

Brizzi started off the cross-examination of Brian by going over his testimony. Brian claimed he forgot that he even had the gun on him, and only remembered it when it almost fell out when he went over the guardrail. He said the gun belonged to his father and he only took it because he didn't want to get Lona or her mother in trouble by leaving it there. He also claimed that he didn't know a police officer was right behind him when he fired the shots, but just shot over his shoulder in the hope that the gunfire would scare anyone from chasing him.

"Well, if that's what you want the jury to believe," Brizzi asked, "why didn't you shoot the gun up in the air?"

"I don't know," Brian responded. "I could have done that."

"You could have shot into the ground, couldn't you?"

"You're right."

"You could have shot the buildings; you could have shot the houses on either side, couldn't you?"

"I could have."

"But you didn't!" Brizzi said with emphasis.

"No."

Judge Borges then said that she had a question from one of the jurors. "Did you or do you have any hearing loss in your left ear?"

"No."

The defense then posed a few more questions on redirect examination to Brian but didn't bring up anything significant.

On recross examination, Brizzi had Brian retell the story about meeting Gary Rees. Brian admitted telling him everything Rees said he had told him, except the part about saying he'd shot the officer intentionally. Brizzi kept hammering Brian with questions about what he'd testified to, and Brian became flustered and said, "You're turning things around and I'm confused now."

Brizzi apparently wanted the jury to think that Brian's whole testimony was confused, so he ended his recross. Once Brizzi had finished with his questioning of Brian, the defense said that it rested its case, and the judge ended the testimony for the day.

The next morning, November 10, 2009, the prosecution recalled Lona Bishop to the witness stand as a rebuttal witness. After Lona received the admonishment that she was still under oath, deputy prosecutor Denise Robinson asked her if she and Brian had, as he'd testified to, smoked two eight balls on July 9, 2008. She said no because those cost $150.00 each. They didn't have the money.

"If you had had the money for it," Robinson asked, "would you have smoked it?"

"Yes."

Earlier, Brian had testified that the .38 caliber revolver he carried had belonged to his father, so Robinson asked Lona, "Can you tell the court when you saw that gun?"

"July 10th and July 9th."

"Where?"

"At my house."

"And who," Robinson asked, "had that gun?"

"Brian."

"Did you see that gun with Paul [Reese Sr.]?"

"No."

"Did Brian carry a gun?"

"Yes."

"How often?"

"I mean all the time."

"On July 10, 2008," Robinson continued, "when Brian opened the door and saw the police standing outside, did he know he was a homicide suspect?"

"Yes."

At this point, once the judge had the jury leave the courtroom, defense attorney David Shircliff again asked for a mistrial because information about an unrelated homicide had been introduced. The judge once more denied the motion.

The prosecution said it had no more questions of Lona Bishop and no more rebuttal witnesses to call. The judge then told the attorneys to prepare for closing arguments.

Prosecutor Denise Robinson started first with the State's closing argument. She carefully went through all of the evidence the State had presented, and how it showed that Brian Reese had intentionally tried to kill Officer Jason Fishburn. She finished her closing argument by saying, "Is it reasonable, is it credible, to believe that the defendant fires blindly at nothing and somehow Jason Fishburn runs around the corner and runs into those bullets? No. We ask you to find him guilty."

Shircliff handled the closing argument for the defense. "I've never asked you to like Brian Reese," he told the jury. "I've never asked you to think the behavior he engaged in is something you'd want to behave like, or that you liked the behavior or that you condoned it or agreed with it. The life he lives is not one that you or I live."

He went on and didn't deny that Brian Reese had fired the shots that struck Fishburn, but insisted that it was an unintentional act and that Brian should be found guilty of aggravated battery rather than attempt murder.

"It's not about intentional murder or intent to murder," Shircliff said. "It's about fleeing. It's about Brian Reese making a bad decision. It's about Brian Reese shooting his gun. Hold him responsible for what he's done and that would be Aggravated Battery. Thank you."

In the State's rebuttal closing argument, the prosecution told the jurors, "Hold him accountable. Tell him he's not in control anymore. He's guilty of Attempt Murder."

Following the closing arguments, the judge gave the jury their instructions as to how the law applied in this case. Once they had these, she sent them to the jury room to deliberate.

The case took a little over a week and went to the jury on Tuesday, November 10, 2009. There is always some uncertainty while a jury is out, because no one knows how they viewed the evidence. What often appears as convincing to the prosecutor or defense attorney may not be that convincing to the jurors. And so both sides waited nervously for the verdicts to be read. But while it had taken a little over a week to try the case, it only took the jurors ninety minutes to find Brian Reese guilty on all counts, including attempt murder, resisting law enforcement, and carrying a handgun without a license.

Shircliff asked for the jurors to be polled. Each one said that they agreed with the verdict. The jury then had to go back into deliberations to decide if Brian Reese should be found guilty of carrying a handgun without a license as a Class D felony or the higher and more serious Class C felony. The jurors were allowed to see his criminal record when they did this. They came back with a recommendation of the Class C felony.

Naturally, the prosecution and the Fishburn family were elated at the verdict. "We were really relieved at the conviction," said Tonya. "We felt we could put this behind us now and move on with our lives."

"We felt we had hit a home run and were really pleased with the verdict," Dennis Fishburn added. "We finally had some closure."

When asked what he thought had tipped the case in their favor, prosecutor Carl Brizzi pointed to Brian's own testimony. "I think the defendant taking the stand tipped it in our favor," he told a reporter for the Indy Channel. "I don't think he was credible. I think he came across as very rehearsed and couldn't answer the tough questions."

Detective Sergeant Jeff Breedlove said he felt that Gary Rees's testimony had made the difference. "Gary Rees really made the case as far as Brian Reese's intent was concerned," he said.

Deputy prosecutor Denise Robinson felt that it was the totality of the evidence that had convicted Brian Reese. "The defense argued that Reese had recklessly and randomly fired at Officer Fishburn and that, therefore, there was no specific intent to kill," she said. "By introducing evidence in a number of seemingly unrelated areas we were able to negate this argument and prove that the shooting was intentional. We introduced testimony on officer training—specifically training relating to the use of Tasers and of firearms—to show the jury that Officer Fishburn was pursuing a known homicide suspect and initially drew and used his Taser, and then, only when faced with deadly force, drew his Glock. We also introduced testimony as to ballistics, firearms trajectory, and the speed at which the bullets of the caliber fired by Reese travelled to show that the injuries sustained by Officer Fishburn had to have been the result of shots intentionally fired."

The jury apparently agreed with prosecutor Carl Brizzi and deputy prosecutor Denise Robinson's assessment. Juror Jim Waters told an Indy Channel reporter, "It came up to us if we believed what [Brian Reese] said, because it was only two people that had saw what happened. Since [Jason Fishburn] couldn't speak for himself, all we had to go by was the defendant and it just wasn't believable."

On December 4, 2009, Judge Lisa Borges held the sentencing hearing for Brian Reese. At these hearings, victims and family members of victims can speak. Dennis Fishburn, Jason's father, told the court, "No one wins in this devastating case, nobody wins. Now it's time to pay the piper, Mr. Reese. They say that forgiveness is the key that unlocks the handcuffs of hate. I've lost that key. I can't find it. Judge, it's in your hands, but while the defense attorney might ask for leniency, I hope you will boldly say, 'Not today.'"

Jason Fishburn also addressed the court. He said, "I can't draw anymore, no more running, no more hiking, no more everything. Brian, I forgive you, but at the same time justice must be served, and I just ask that the sentence is the fullest."

Family members and friends of the person convicted can also say a few words at the sentencing hearing. Amy Brackin, the mother of three of Brian's children, told the court what an absolutely wonderful man Brian was. Richard Ward, a friend and fellow window washer, told the judge what a great, nonviolent person Brian was. Two of Brian's daughters, Stephanie and Amanda, also testified and said what a wonderful, loving father Brian was, and how tough it would be on them if he was sent away for a long time.

Following this testimony, Judge Borges sentenced Brian to the maximum sentence possible: fifty-nine years in prison. He received fifty years for attempt murder, one year for resisting law enforcement, and eight years for carrying a handgun without a license. The judge ordered the sentences to be served consecutively. She told Brian, "If you take a gun in your hand and you point it at a police officer and you pull the trigger, then you have cut down something that is the fabric of our lives."

Dennis Fishburn couldn't have been happier with the sentence. "Being a police officer and a father, I definitely didn't want to see anything other than guilty and the maximum sentence. And we got it."

As often happens, Brian Reese eventually appealed his conviction in the Officer Jason Fishburn shooting. He based his appeal on what he believed were four mistakes made by the court.

1. That the court abused its discretion by admitting evidence of uncharged bad acts in violation of Indiana Evidence Rule 404(b).

2. That the court abused its discretion in instructing the jury.
3. That there was insufficient evidence to support his conviction for attempt murder.
4. That he had been improperly sentenced.

As for the first point of his appeal, Brian noted that a detective testifying at his trial had identified himself as a homicide detective. He also directed the appeals court's attention to the testimony of another police officer who told the court that he had been dispatched at the request of Homicide. Brian claimed that the testimony of these two police officers had tainted the jury by letting them know that he was a murder suspect. Indiana Evidence Rule 404(b), he said, didn't allow testimony about charges or convictions unrelated to the case at hand. The appeals court, however, didn't agree. They pointed out that Lona Bishop had testified that Brian knew he was a murder suspect when he ran from the police. Along with this, the court said, Brian himself had opened the door to the testimony he objected to by telling the jury that he thought the police were chasing him because of a theft warrant he had out on him and "because I was running around with a gun in my hand."

Brian's second point of appeal, about the faulty jury instruction, he based on his objection to the judge's instruction: "The intent to kill may be inferred from the nature of the attack and the circumstances surrounding the crime." Brian claimed that the word "attack" was prejudicial to him, that it made the incident appear to be an intentional act, rather than unintentional as he claimed. The appeals court again disagreed. They said that, at most, the court had made only a "harmless error" in using the word "attack" in the jury instruction, particularly in light of testimony that Brian had fired multiple shots at Officer Fishburn, two of them striking him with "deadly accuracy."

On the third point of Brian's appeal, that there was insufficient evidence presented at his trial to convict him of attempt murder, the appeals court once more disagreed. They said, "The requisite intent to commit murder may be inferred from the intentional use of a deadly weapon in a manner likely to cause death" and that "discharging a weapon in the direction of a victim is substantial evidence from which a jury can infer intent to kill." Additionally, the appeals court pointed out that Gary Rees had testified that Brian had claimed he'd ambushed the officer. The appeals court said they felt that the jury had sufficient evidence for their decision.

On Brian's claim that his sentence was too harsh, specifically that his four children (one with Lona Bishop and three with Amy Brackin) would no longer have his support, the appeals court continued to disagree. In their written opinion, they said that, according to case law: "A trial court is not required to find that a defendant's incarceration would result in undue hardship upon his dependants" and "many persons convicted of serious crimes have one or more children and, absent special circumstances, trial courts are not required to find that imprisonment would result in an undue hardship." But in addition to this, the appeals court also noted that Brian's parental rights with Lona Bishop had already been terminated, and that the other three children had received only minimal support from Brian over the years. His imprisonment wouldn't have that much financial impact on them.

Brian also claimed that his sentence, which was the maximum possible, had been inappropriate for him. The appeals court noted, however, that Officer Fishburn had attempted to stop Brian with verbal commands and the use of his Taser, and that Brian had responded to this with deadly force, ambushing Fishburn and critically wounding him. Also, the court noted, Brian had a long criminal history as both a juvenile and an adult. In addition, he had previously violated his probation, was out on bond when he shot Officer Fishburn, and had a history of drug abuse. The appeals court stated, "In sum, there is nothing in the nature of the offenses or the character of the offender to persuade us that a maximum sentence is inappropriate."

The following year, on October 25, 2010, Brian Reese was scheduled to go to trial for the murder of Clifford Haddix, but he apparently realized the futility of it, and instead of going to trial, on October 22, 2010, Brian Reese pleaded guilty. The evidence against him in the case had been overwhelming. Homicide detectives had discovered that Lona Bishop, along with Paul Reese Sr., had accompanied Brian to Haddix's house and that Paul Sr. had acted as a lookout, talking with Brian over a walkie-talkie.

The police had arrested Lona, and eventually charged her with conspiracy to commit robbery. Since she had no criminal record at all, the police had believed that there was a good chance they could get her to testify against Brian and Paul Reese Sr. in order to keep from going to prison herself. Her attorney would tell a reporter for the Indy Channel that "Lona intends to fully cooperate with the Prosecutor's Office." She did, and eventually pleaded guilty to conspiracy to commit robbery. She received a twenty-year sentence, but because of her cooperation with the police, the judge (over the objection of deputy prosecutor Denise Robinson) suspended the sentence and placed her on probation.

Brian's father, Paul Reese Sr., also agreed to cooperate with the police. Although originally arrested for murder, robbery, burglary, and being a habitual criminal, Paul Sr. made a deal with the prosecutor to plead guilty to burglary in the Haddix case, and received a twenty-year sentence in exchange for his cooperation.

And so, following his guilty plea in the Haddix case and the fact that his father and girlfriend had both become State's Witnesses, Brian really had no choice but to also plead guilty to the murders of Demetrius Allen and Crystal Joy Jenkins, crimes he had been charged with on July 16, 2008. The gun he'd already been convicted of using in the Officer Jason Fishburn shooting had been used in Allen's murder as well. On December 16, 2010, a judge sentenced Brian to 189 years in prison for the three murders. According to his Department of Corrections fact sheet, his earliest possible release date is July 6, 2132.

Deputy prosecutor Denise Robinson added some final thoughts about the Brian Reese case. "As for Brian Reese, in addition to convicting him of shooting Officer Fishburn, he was also convicted of three homicides, and he will be in prison for the remainder of his life," she said. "Jason Fishburn is a fine young man who wanted nothing more than to be a police officer and Brian Reese took that from him. Nothing I did can restore Jason's life and career to him. In the end, all I could do was hold Brian Reese accountable."

It appeared that one member of the Reese family, at least, would never again be free to harm anyone.

ELEVEN

In the years following thirteen-year-old Dawn Marie Stuard's murder in 1986, her father Ted Stuard tried his best to deal with what had happened in a way that allowed him to function on a day-to-day basis. "To maintain my sanity, I tried over the years to put a lot of it out of my mind," he said. "I tried not to think about it, but if I did, I tried to remember the good things so that I could repress the bad things. I could still hear that goofy little girl laugh of hers," he added with a sad smile. Unfortunately, he found that his method of trying to block it out didn't work nearly as well as he would have liked it to. "But the bad times outweighed the good, and so I just tried not to remember too much."

For the first few years after Dawn's murder, Ted went through a lot of despair and grief, a lot of simply not believing that it could have happened. A dark depression soon followed. "He said that he grieved most for the lost opportunity of watching his daughter grow up and for all the opportunities she would never have," said WXIN reporter Russ McQuaid. Small things—like hearing a certain song, or the sound of a little girl laughing, or seeing a character in a movie—would remind him of Dawn, and then all the feelings of despair and grief would rush back.

Ted's wife, Sandy, didn't fare any better after Dawn's murder, and eventually their marriage broke up, a not uncommon result in such circumstances. Eventually, both of them got remarried to other people, but even moving on to a new marriage couldn't reduce the anguish Ted felt. He found that the only method that worked for him was to simply close off that portion of his life, to try not to think about it. And so, he tried to blank out his mind about everything that had happened and to just get through each day without dwelling on it. He became numb.

He didn't even share it with his new wife, Linda, for almost seven years after they were married. "Linda didn't even know about Dawn for a long time," Ted said. "She didn't know that I'd had a daughter murdered. She didn't know anything because I didn't talk about it."

Linda, however, could tell that Ted had something traumatic in his past, something that haunted him, something he kept all bottled up inside. She could tell that he was hurting but didn't want to push him into talking about it. She decided to just let it come out naturally when he felt it was time to talk.

"For the first seven years we were married," said Linda

Stuard, "he didn't say anything about Dawn." She wasn't completely in the dark, though. "His family would tell me things. But I didn't push the subject because I knew that when he was ready to talk about it he would."

And yet, even though Ted Stuard fought desperately to keep his sanity by not thinking about what had happened to his little girl, he couldn't help but think of Dawn every year on her birthday. And every time St. Patrick's Day rolled around, he felt sick all over, as if his chest cavity had suddenly filled with dark, icy water, because he couldn't help but think of what had happened to his daughter on that day in 1986.

"St. Patrick's Day became a very dreaded holiday for me," said Ted Stuard. "Whenever it got close to the anniversary of Dawn's death, of course she would come to mind."

In addition to the depression, Ted Stuard also had to deal with the anger. A man had murdered his daughter yet walked around free. A man who everyone knew was a criminal had choked his daughter to death, after sexually assaulting her, yet it seemed that nothing could be done about it. Paul Reese Sr. was still a free man, out in the world hurting who knew how many more people. Ted would become consumed by the unfairness of the situation. It just wasn't right: an evil man getting away with killing an innocent little girl.

"After over twenty years, Reese was still on the street and my daughter was in the ground," Ted said. "The less I thought about it, the better I could handle the stress. But still sometimes I just couldn't help but remember."

To get by, he would fantasize about how Paul Reese Sr.'s own death would occur. Of course, the police were well aware of these kinds of thoughts, and they had warned Ted against acting on them.

"I was told by law enforcement at the time of the murder that if a bolt of lightning came down and struck Mr. Reese in the head, and there were ten witnesses standing around, that they would still investigate me," Ted recalled. "They told me I couldn't get away with it, so don't do it."

After years of depression and anguish, however, Ted Stuard knew he had to somehow find a way to deal with the terrible memories of what had happened to his daughter. He found himself becoming physically ill whenever he thought about how he had failed Dawn, about how he should have been there to protect her. Of course, he also knew that no one could have foreseen what had happened, but that didn't stop the guilt. The only thing that got him through it was hoping that someday something would happen in the case, that some new witness or piece of evidence would appear, anything that could bring about an arrest and a trial, and perhaps give him some closure. Then maybe it wouldn't hurt so much.

But the years slipped by and nothing new happened with the case. It went cold and stayed cold. "Any chance I got, I tried to bring Dawn's case back up to the public interest," said Ted Stuard. "I hoped that maybe somebody would think, 'Oh, that hasn't been solved yet? I know something about that case.' I did anything that I thought could kick start the case. Of course, this just brought the old memories back."

Ted was willing to deal with all of the grief and despair, with all of the depression and anger, if it would just get something done about his daughter's murder. He desperately wanted someone to come forward with new evidence or new testimony. He wanted Paul Reese Sr. to be held accountable. But as the years passed and no one came forward, the case stayed unsolved. As the 1980s, the 1990s, and most of the first decade of the twenty-first century passed without any changes in Dawn's case, Ted began to lose hope that her murder investigation would ever be revived. He began to believe that he would never see justice for his daughter.

But then, in July 2008, when the police arrested Brian Reese for the shooting of Officer Jason Fishburn, and then arrested Brian and Paul Reese Sr. for the robbery and murder of Clifford Haddix, Ted found that his years of trying to bring Dawn's case back to the public's attention finally bore fruit when Russ McQuaid, a reporter for the local Fox affiliate WXIN, researched the case, found out about the connection to Dawn's murder, and requested an interview with Ted Stuard. Ted, of course, was glad to give the interview. This was the best opportunity he had seen in decades to have his daughter's murder investigation reopened by the police.

"Ted Stuard told me that he had always suspected Paul Reese Sr., and that he even confronted him about it the day after Dawn disappeared," said McQuaid. The story about Dawn's murder then appeared on the local

Fox evening news. Soon other news media outlets also picked up the story, and although talking about it was painful, Ted did several more interviews with the news media about Dawn's case. Again, he hoped that the exposure would pressure someone with information to come forward. Ted had always felt certain that there was someone, somewhere, with the information they needed to convict Paul Reese Sr. for the murder of his daughter.

But despite everything he did, despite the reopening of old wounds, nothing of significance came of all this publicity. The old despair and hopelessness, like a flood raging behind a breaking dam, felt ready at any second to burst forward and drown him. Because his hopes had been raised so high with the arrests of the Reeses, Ted didn't know if he could go back to his old method of not thinking about Dawn and what had happened to her. He didn't know if he could block it out anymore. Too many things now reminded him of Dawn.

"I was at a wedding, and they played my daughter's favorite song," said Ted Stuard. "It'd been twenty-three or twenty-four years by that time. The song started it all back up again."

The feelings simply couldn't stay repressed any longer. It was just too much to bear. Fortunately, Ted's wife, Linda, could see what was happening to her husband and decided in 2011 to take over his efforts to get the case reopened. She had witnessed the despair and grief Ted had gone through for so many years and knew that she had to do something and do it quickly. Even though Ted had been quiet about Dawn's murder for a long, long time, she realized that the incident had suddenly come back alive for her husband, and also realized that it would drive him into even deeper depression if it wasn't somehow resolved.

"Linda saw how I was acting and feeling," said Ted Stuard. "She said that we couldn't afford to lose another person to the Reeses. She told me to settle down and let her see what she could do about the case."

"I just didn't want this case pushed back again," said Linda Stuard. "What with the Reeses getting arrested for those other murders, I knew that the time to go forward with Dawn's case was now."

She knew that the detectives in 1986 had also been certain that Paul Reese Sr. was involved in Dawn's murder. Now, with the recent turmoil over the three murders and the shooting of Officer Fishburn, it just added more support to the idea that Paul Reese Sr. and maybe other members of his family had been involved in Dawn's death. Linda called the Homicide Branch of the Indianapolis Metropolitan Police Department and was transferred to the Cold Case Squad.

Linda spoke with cold case detective Mark Albert, who, like the entire Indianapolis Metropolitan Police Department, naturally knew about the Reeses and their recent troubles with the law. It wasn't a far stretch for him to believe that they might have been involved in another murder. After they had talked for a bit, Detective Albert told Linda that he would pull out Dawn's case file and see if there was anything that could be done.

"I had just solved a thirty-year-old murder case, and was looking for another good cold case to work on. I didn't know anything about Dawn's murder, but I told her that I would pull up the case file and have a look at it," said Detective Mark Albert.

Naturally, the relatives of all murder victims whose cases had gone cold want their loved one's investigation reopened and solved. But detectives who investigate homicide cold cases know that success in their field comes only rarely. Reopening a case was by no means a guarantee that it would eventually lead to an arrest and a conviction in court. Still, Detective Albert felt that it was certainly worth looking into this case, especially with all of the recent troubles the Reeses had been in.

"Mark told me to give him just a little time," said Linda Stuard. "He said that he didn't know anything about Dawn or her case, but that he would look into it."

When Detective Albert pulled out the Dawn Marie Stuard case file, he saw that the investigation had originally been assigned to Detective Sergeant Roy West. He knew Roy West well. West was retired now but had also worked for a short time on the police department's Cold Case Squad, though on a different shift. And so, Detective Albert contacted West and spoke with him about the case, which West remembered vividly.

"Roy told me that he wanted to solve this case more than any other case he'd ever had," said Detective Albert. "He said that he had never forgotten about it."

After reading the case file, Detective Albert felt that perhaps something could be done with the investigation, but that he needed to give the case a little push. Like Ted, he thought it might help to give the investigation some publicity. The public needed to know that the case was still unsolved, that the murderer of a thirteen-year-old girl still walked around free.

"I knew we needed to get some publicity on this case so that people who might not have wanted to talk about the case in 1986 would remember it and perhaps be willing to talk about it now," said Albert. He drove Ted and Linda Stuard to WIBC Talk Radio and had them do an interview, and also scheduled them to appear on a radio call-in show hosted by county prosecutor Carl Brizzi.

"We have over eight hundred cases in our homicide cold case file," said Detective Albert. "This one just stuck out for some reason. Ted Stuard went on Prosecutor Brizzi's radio show and gave such a passionate plea for help that the other media outlets picked up on the case, and as a result a really important witness came forward."

It was a new step forward, but the case was still a long way from being closed.

TWELVE

While one occasionally hears about a murder case that is twenty, thirty, or even forty years old finally being solved, and the perpetrator convicted and sent to prison, these are the rare cases, which is why they make the news. The truth is that most homicide cold cases go cold for very good reasons: lack of evidence, lack of reliable witnesses, lack of a body, or a thousand other possible causes for failure. Resurrecting a case is often nothing but an exercise in frustration and futility both for the police and the families of the victims. There may still be no evidence, still no reliable witnesses, or still no body. The cases are simply not workable.

The Indianapolis Metropolitan Police Department had over eight hundred cases in its homicide cold case file. These are unsolved murder cases from a certain date forward, using a date so that detectives can assume the murderer and/or possible witnesses are still alive. The number eight hundred is fairly typical and proportionately true for every other city in the United States. According to an article in the June 2004 issue of the magazine *Law Enforcement Technology*, in 2004 there were over 200,000 unsolved murders in the United States since 1960, with 6,000 new unsolved murders being added every year.

So how many out of these eight hundred cold cases will the Indianapolis cold case detectives solve? The Cold Case Squad considers itself a great success if it solves two or three cases a year. Unlike new cases with fresh evidence, these are cases that have already been thoroughly worked over by homicide detectives and then "deactivated" because the detectives at the time were unable to collect the evidence or witness statements necessary for an arrest—they are cases detectives thought would likely never be solved. Any case that they felt stood a decent chance of being solved would never have been deactivated in the first place. Again, this success rate of two or three cases a year is proportionately true for cities across the United States. Therefore, it doesn't take a lot of mathematics to see that, when one compares the total number of homicide cold cases with the success rate, most homicide cold cases will never be solved.

Unlike regular homicide detectives, who simply take every new investigation they are assigned and work with its new witnesses and new information to try to solve the case, homicide cold case detectives are following someone else's work: what clues were followed, what witnesses were talked to, and how the crime scene was searched. Cold case detectives don't get the chance to look at the crime scene right after the murder, and they don't get the chance to talk to witnesses while their memories are still fresh. Instead, cold case detectives must try to figure out what the original detectives may have missed, or what evidence can now be scientifically analyzed that couldn't be when the case was new. Cold case work is mostly a lot of dry research and a lot of rereading of old homicide case files. The work can be slow, tedious, and often frustrating, with only an occasional victory, and not all detectives are suited to it. As retired Miami Detective Sergeant David Rivers, who headed Miami's Homicide Cold Case Squad, said, "We discussed who would come into the squad and we all agreed not all homicide detectives would make good cold case detectives. Action doesn't come fast and furious. There has to be a pragmatic approach."

Similarly, not all cold cases are suited for reexamination. Cold case detectives carefully review the homicide files in order to determine which ones may have a chance of now being solved—to try to work on every single homicide cold case would waste millions of man hours every year across the nation. How are those cases, the ones that cold case detectives do decide to look into, chosen? What would make a homicide cold case like the Dawn Marie Stuard case, which had in the past already been thoroughly investigated, suddenly viable?

There are a number of factors that figure into why a homicide cold case detective will decide to reopen a case and try to solve it. One of the things homicide cold case detectives look for in an old murder investigation is a change in relationships, such as former lovers or spouses. While a person may have been deeply in love when he or she gave a murder suspect an alibi, this person may now be estranged and possibly even openly hostile to the suspect. The estranged individual may have given the murder suspect an alibi that he or she now wants to recant, or has some facts about the case that he or she withheld at the time of the original investigation, information that he or she is now willing to share. That person could now fill the detective's ear with good information that will lead to an arrest.

It can also often be worthwhile to talk again with witnesses not as closely attached to a murder suspect as a lover or spouse but who might recall things that for some reason didn't come up during the original investigation, yet that may now appear crucial to the homicide cold case detective. The witnesses' relationships with a murder suspect may also have changed over the years. At the time of the original investigation the witnesses may have been afraid to tell the detectives what happened for fear of retaliation, or it may have been that they thought the suspect was innocent and they were trying to help him or her. The passing years can diminish the fear or bring these witnesses to the realization that the suspect likely wasn't innocent after all. Also, witnesses may have had a religious conversion since the murder and suddenly feel guilty about not sharing information with the police that they know they should have.

And of course, in any homicide cold case, it can sometimes be helpful to just have a new set of eyes look at the investigation. Sometimes the original homicide detectives became too close to an investigation, or became so convinced that a certain person was the murderer, that they couldn't see the importance of other evidence. This tunnel vision may have led them to dismiss other suspects, or—even unintentionally—overlook or ignore important evidence that didn't agree with their belief. A new set of eyes looking at the case can often see directions that the case should have gone in originally, but didn't.

But by far the biggest help to homicide cold case detectives comes from the many recent scientific breakthroughs and ever-improving technology that brings with it new methods of analyzing evidence and identifying criminals. Over the last few decades, science has stunningly improved upon computer systems, chemical processes, microscopes, spectrometers, and other scientific equipment. Evidence that twenty or thirty years ago couldn't be analyzed or identified suddenly now can be.

For example, advances in alternate light sources and chemicals have allowed investigators to locate blood that would have been impossible to find in the past. Chemicals such as luminol and fluorescein can detect both new and old blood at a crime scene. They are sprayed on an area, and then a technician, using a special light and goggles, will see either a bluish glow for luminol or a greenish white glow for fluorescein wherever there is blood, even though the suspect may have tried to clean it up. It is also possible to use a special ultraviolet light source to detect blood, even on walls that have been painted over.

The emergence of national databases has also proved invaluable. For instance, the Bureau of Alcohol, Tobacco, Firearms and Explosives (ATF) now maintains a national link between state computer systems that hold information about markings on bullets and bullet casings. Called the National Integrated Ballistic Information Network, or NIBIN, this system can be accessed by any police department in the United States.

One of the most important scientific advances in closing both old and new homicide cases, however, has been the Automated Fingerprint Identification System, or AFIS. Prior to the introduction of AFIS into law enforcement in the mid-1980s, the recovery of even an excellent fingerprint at a crime scene could often prove useless if the police didn't have a known suspect to compare the fingerprint against. There was simply no practical way to manually check it against the often millions of individual fingerprints most large cities had on file. Consequently, if a recovered fingerprint in a murder investigation didn't match anyone already known to be involved in the case, it simply went into the case file, and that was that. It would only be looked at again if a new suspect came up in the case.

"Officers would go to a crime scene and throw [fingerprint] powder around and make the complainant think they were doing something," Peggy Jones, a fingerprint examiner for the Houston Police Department said in an interview in the September 12, 1985, issue of the *Los Angeles Times*. "But then the prints would be filed away never to be touched again unless a suspect was developed." AFIS changed this by allowing officers to use computers that digitized fingerprints and then not only stored this digitized information in their memories, but also compared this new digitized fingerprint against the fingerprints already stored in their memories. And most important of all, it could do this in minutes rather than the years it would have taken if done manually.

Because a fingerprint recovered from a crime scene is seldom as good a quality as a fingerprint taken with ink and a finger roll at a police station, an AFIS computer doesn't give just one match to a evidentiary fingerprint, but offers a batch from its memory with characteristics similar to the evidentiary fingerprint. A fingerprint technician must then compare the AFIS results to the evidentiary fingerprint and find the one that matches. Usually, the matching fingerprint is among the first few on the list.

Ultimately, AFIS became the most important advance in law enforcement detection since the introduction of fingerprints into law enforcement in the early part of the twentieth century. It then became even more valuable when the FBI, in 1999, established IAFIS, its national link of state AFIS computers. What this meant was that, starting around the turn of the twenty-first century, a fingerprint recovered at a crime scene in California could now be matched to the fingerprints taken from a person who had been arrested in New York or Florida.

Yet, while AFIS has been a huge boon to law enforcement, helping the police to identify thousands and thousands of criminals, it has also become extremely valuable for homicide cold case detectives. Now cold case detectives, when combing through homicides prior to the introduction of AFIS, have started looking for cases where unknown fingerprints had been recovered by the police but simply filed away because the detectives didn't have a suspect. Homicide cold case detectives can now run these fingerprints through AFIS and very possibly turn up a suspect in a cold case murder, where before there had been none.

AFIS has also been used by the police to identify murder victims in cases where the victims' fingerprints were on file, and the system has continued to expand its capabilities to now include all joints of the finger and also palm prints. As might be expected, this improvement in AFIS has helped tremendously in solving both new and cold cases. "Under the new, advanced system, AFIS now has the ability to match prints from all areas of the finger and palm," said King County prosecuting attorney Daniel T. Satterberg in an October 10, 2011, press release.

Along with AFIS, the introduction of the personal

computer, and with it the use of the Internet, has been of tremendous help to detectives. Cold case investigators can use the power of their computers to look for patterns, crunch numbers, or use software packages that can sort, collate, and display information into patterns the original detectives may not have seen. Also, software is now available that creates a 3-D rendering of a crime scene, allowing cold case detectives the chance to "see" an old crime scene. The Internet also allows detectives to now have instant access to records and information, including information unavailable at the time of the original investigation. Detectives can now also pull up records from other states, or find personal information on individuals involved in the case via various government websites, organizational websites, and even through social interaction websites such as Facebook.

In addition to all of this, the Internet now also allows police agencies to share information like never before. The 9/11 tragedy brought about this new effort among police departments to share information, some of the effort voluntary and some of it mandated. However, along with regional sharing, information sharing about cold case homicide investigation can also now occur on a national level. As an example of this, the FBI manages a program called the Violent Criminal Apprehension Program, or ViCAP. This is the largest repository of facts about homicides in the United States. Police agencies from all across the nation can send information about a homicide to ViCAP, which then makes the information available to all police agencies nationwide. Homicide cold case detectives will often use ViCAP to see if any of the cases on file there match the case they are investigating.

According to the U.S. Department of Justice's *The Victim's Voice*, "The information is accepted at ViCAP, checked for accuracy, and becomes part of an increasingly comprehensive data bank of homicides that will always be available for comparing and tracking serial offenders. The case information is then compared to other cases in the data bank for similarities in physical, informational, and behavioral characteristics."

Along with ViCAP, in 2003 the Naval Criminal Investigative Service (NCIS) launched a program called the Law Enforcement Information Exchange, or LInX. Much like ViCAP, LInX lets law enforcement agencies exchange information about crimes and criminals. Members of LInX can search the computer database for information about crimes similar to the ones they are investigating.

All of these technological advances, however, pale in comparison to the one that has assisted law enforcement in identifying more suspects, and homicide cold case detectives in solving more decades-old cases, than any other: the introduction of DNA analysis into law enforcement. DNA, of course, is the body's blueprint, a copy of which is contained in almost every cell of the body, and which can be obtained from skin cells, saliva, blood, semen, and many other bodily fluids.

What is so great about DNA analysis for homicide cold case investigations, besides being able to positively identify the owner of almost any bodily substance left behind at a crime scene, is that items properly stored at a police facility can now be tested for DNA even decades after a crime. DNA, it has been found, can remain intact and testable for many years. Crime lab technicians have been able to analyze these decades-old DNA samples and positively link them to a specific person, much as AFIS has with fingerprints.

For example, on December 10, 2003, police officers in Wauwatosa, Wisconsin, solved a 1958 rape and murder with the arrest of eighty-two-year-old John Watson. Homicide cold case detectives who decided to look into the rape and murder found the victim's pajamas still stored away in their property room. Crime lab technicians managed to obtain DNA from semen still on the evidence after forty-five years. The suspect in the case, incidentally, was well known to the police, having been suspected in a number of cases that involved attacks on women.

"It was kind of eerie to see all that," homicide detective Lisa Hudson said in an article in the February 2004 issue of *Evidence Technology Magazine*. "I opened the box and there were her bloody pajamas and the bedding, preserved."

The use of DNA analysis has become so widespread and pervasive in law enforcement that states have set up DNA banks, in which DNA samples taken from criminals arrested in the state are kept, and which can be used when looking for a match to DNA recovered at a crime scene. All states now have laws requiring the collection of DNA from certain arrested individuals, which then goes into that state's DNA bank. But the search can go even wider than just state boundaries. The FBI, in 1990, formed the Combined DNA Index System, or CODIS. At that time it was just a pilot project and had only twelve law enforcement agencies participating. Today, police agencies from every state send DNA samples to CODIS, so that a DNA sample taken from a crime scene in Denver can now be matched to a criminal who lives in Tampa.

An example of this occurred in September 2012 in Redding, California. On August 10, 1991, Redding police found the body of fifty-three-year-old Despina Magioudis lying in a field. Someone had beaten, strangled, and raped her. Although the police thoroughly investigated this case, the body went to the morgue and the case went cold and stayed cold until homicide cold case detectives got a hit on DNA from the crime. Forty-five-year-old Brian Eric Norton had been convicted of raping a woman in Iowa in 2007. As a condition of his conviction, the state of Iowa took a DNA sample from Norton (usually done by running a cotton swab inside the cheek) and entered Norton's DNA into CODIS. The police in Redding, using CODIS, were able to identify Norton as the killer of Despina Magioudis.

The above case, along with showing the power of DNA, also shows the importance of homicide cold case detectives occasionally resubmitting fingerprints or DNA for comparison in cold cases. While the sample may not match anyone on the first submission, as it wouldn't have done with Norton in 2006, new information and samples are constantly coming into these data banks.

In a case similar to Dawn Marie Stuard's, Indianapolis homicide Detective Sergeant Mike Crooke's first unsolved case involved the rape and murder of fifteen-year-old Tracey Poindexter. On April 13, 1985, a caller notified the police of a body in a creek on the north side of Indianapolis, and Detective Sergeant Crooke responded to the scene. The victim, it appeared, had been raped before being murdered and dumped in the creek. Detective Sergeant Crooke thoroughly investigated the case, including collecting a sample of the semen recovered from Tracey's body during the autopsy, and finally sending the sample to the property room for storage when the case went cold. In 1985, the semen sample, without a known suspect, held little evidentiary value. And even if they had had a suspect in 1985, the most the crime lab could have said was whether he did or did not fall within a group of men that could have produced this semen; helpful but hardly definitive evidence. Since the case had involved such a young victim, though, it had stuck with Detective Sergeant Crooke. He could never forget it or ever give up hope of someday being able to solve it.

In 2001, Detective Sergeant Crooke attended a conference where one of the speakers talked about CODIS, and about how DNA from things such as semen could now be positively matched to a specific individual. As soon as he got back to Indianapolis, Crooke got the semen sample out of the property room and sent it in for a DNA analysis. The sample matched a man named Sterling Riggs, who had just gotten out of prison after serving fifteen years for a kidnapping and rape very similar to the Tracey Poindexter case. In November 2001, a jury found Riggs guilty of Tracey Poindexter's rape and murder, and soon afterward a judge sentenced Riggs to 130 years in prison.

In a similar case, in September 2011, the police in Englewood, Colorado, finally closed the murder case of five-year-old Alie Berrelez. Over eighteen years earlier, on May 18, 1993, someone had kidnapped the little girl from the parking lot of the apartment complex where she lived. The police, using tracking dogs, found her body four days later. The murderer had stuffed her into a canvas bag and then dumped her near a creek fourteen miles from where she had been kidnapped. The police immediately suspected a neighbor by the name of Nick Stofer but could never obtain the evidence they needed to arrest him.

The only real evidence the police had on Stofer in 1993 was the testimony of a witness to the kidnapping: Alie's three-year-old brother. He pointed out Stofer's apartment and told the officers that "the old man" who lived there had grabbed Alie. This, though, just wasn't enough to arrest Stofer on. The police and prosecutor knew that a defense attorney would immediately attack the credibility of such a young witness. And so, the case went cold.

"We wanted to put the cuffs on [Stofer] so bad, but we couldn't because the evidence wasn't there," Englewood chief of police John Collins told ABC News on September 13, 2011.

But cold case detectives didn't give up. In 2011, the DNA technology that hadn't been available in 1993 was able to test evidence from the victim's underwear and prove that the DNA belonged to Nick Stofer.

Scientists are also constantly making improvements in DNA technology. When DNA analysis first became available, technicians needed a sample about the size of a quarter in order to analyze it, but over the years the sample size needed for analysis has become smaller and smaller, leading to one of the most useful innovations to date in DNA technology, called "touch DNA." Whenever a person touches something, he or she leaves skin cells behind. Scientists are now able to recover and use these microscopic skin cells to develop a DNA profile and identify the owner. Touch DNA samples can be taken from a telephone, a gun, a knife, a piece of fabric, and practically anything else touched by a suspect. Obviously, this has widened tremendously the scope of DNA analysis.

Despite the remarkable advances that have occurred, however, fiction is always ahead of reality. It has become standard now that in cases that hinge on scientific evidence that prosecutors must first speak to the jury about the "CSI effect." This is because due to the television series *CSI* and other similar programs and movies, many jurors believe that they already know how evidence is collected and analyzed in a criminal case, even though unfortunately, in many of these television programs and films, the information given is wrong or the equipment they use is not real, but simply dreamed up by the writers. Prosecutors have to explain to the jurors that many of the things depicted about crime detection in television and movies are, alas, not true. Several years ago in Indianapolis, for example, homicide detectives had what they felt was an excellent murder case against a suspect and were puzzled when the jury returned with a not guilty verdict. When detectives talked to the jury afterward, one of the jurors said, "Well we knew the police officer was wrong because that's not the way they do it on *NYPD Blue*."

And finally, for homicide cold case detectives stuck on an investigation that they believe can be solved, but just aren't sure how to do it, there are several organizations that can assist. Max Houck, a forensic anthropologist who worked for the FBI and helped in the identification of bodies at the 9/11 site in New York City, formed the nonprofit Institute for Cold Case Evaluation, or ICCE, soon after the 9/11 tragedy. The organization is made up of not just forensic anthropologists, but also chemists, pathologists, entomologists, evidence analysts, and many other forensic specialists. Their mission is to assist police agencies in the investigation of difficult homicide cold cases.

"They're not publicly known names," Houck said in a

September 2003 interview that appeared in the *Burlington County Times* about the personnel who worked for ICCE. "They spend more time in the lab than in front of the camera, but they are the people who really do the work."

Along with ICCE, the Vidocq Society is also available to assist homicide cold case detectives with particularly difficult investigations. The society, headquartered in Philadelphia and founded in 1990, is made up of forensic specialists, including former homicide detectives, prosecutors, scientists from a number of fields, and others who have worked in homicide investigation. They will look at a case and provide guidance to a homicide cold case detective. The society is very selective about the cases it takes but does not charge police departments or the victims' families for its services.

So why aren't more than a handful of homicide cold cases solved every year? In addition to a simple lack of feasible evidence, the reason often comes down to money. Because of budget shortfalls, many police departments are understaffed, with homicide detectives barely able to handle the new homicides that come in. Cold cases are, understandably, low priority. Fortunately, Indianapolis had a very active homicide cold case squad, and also had a former detective like Roy West, who couldn't forget the Dawn Marie Stuard case and had never given up hope of solving it.

And so, following Linda Stuard's and Detective Albert's intervention, Detective Sergeant Roy West began looking once more at the Dawn Marie Stuard case. He

strongly believed that new scientific techniques and innovations would allow the case to be prosecuted. There
was still, he knew, evidence from the murder stored away
that could likely benefit from what science could now do
that it couldn't do in 1986.

THIRTEEN

By the time that Marion County prosecutor Carl Brizzi charged Brian Reese with the robbery and murder of sixty-nine-year-old Clifford Haddix, Brian was already sitting in jail, having been arrested for the attempted murder of Police Officer Jason Fishburn on July 10, 2008.

Brizzi also charged Brian's father, Paul Reese Sr., with murder in the Clifford Haddix case, since the elder Reese had acted as a lookout in this incident. Paul Sr. would later tell the police that he had talked back and forth with Brian over a walkie-talkie while he was in the Haddix house on what Paul Sr. claimed was supposed to be just an ordinary burglary. He reportedly didn't know about or agree with the Haddix murder. However, under Indiana's felony murder law, even though Paul Sr. had stayed outside, he could still be found guilty of murder because he was a part of the criminal act.

Paul Sr., of course, quickly realized that this meant he could spend the rest of his life in prison. And so, in a desperate attempt to avoid this, he began negotiating a plea deal with the prosecutor. He would plead guilty to burglary, receive a twenty-year sentence, and cooperate with the police in their investigation of his son. In Indiana, with its good time rule, which gives prisoners one day off of their sentence for every day of good behavior, the twenty-year sentence meant that Paul Sr. could be paroled and out of prison in ten years or less. (There are also other ways a prisoner can get time taken off of his or her sentence, such as by obtaining a college degree while in prison.) But along with this, in order for Paul Reese Sr. not to be charged with murder, he also had to agree to cooperate with the police in their other homicide investigation against his son, the Demetrius Allen and Crystal Joy Jenkins murders, which he did. Paul Sr. told the police that his son had shot both of them, one with a .38 caliber revolver and the other with a 25 mm. semiautomatic pistol. The bullets from the .38 caliber weapon used in the murders matched the bullets that had struck Officer Fishburn.

Paul Reese Sr. fully cooperated with the police and then pleaded guilty to burglary in the Haddix case. Immediately after this, he began serving his twenty-year sentence at the Pendleton Correction Facility, a maximum security prison in Pendleton, Indiana, about thirty-five miles northeast of Indianapolis.

Ted Stuard, who had revived his daughter's case when the Reeses were all over the news, still waited for justice. In an interview in 2011 with WISH-TV, he said, "The first couple of years are terrible, [and] twenty-four to twenty-five years later it still hurts, you still mourn, you still look for justice."

By 2011, however, justice finally did seem to be a possibility.

As he'd told Detective Mark Albert, Detective Sergeant Roy West had never been able to get the Dawn Marie Stuard case out of his mind. Not only had it been his very first murder investigation, not only had it gone unsolved, but most importantly, it had involved a totally innocent victim. Every few years, West would pull the case file out and have a look at it, hoping that something would jump out at him, something he had overlooked. When DNA testing first began being used in criminal cases in the 1990s, he'd pulled the file only to discover that, in order to do the blood typing in 1986, the crime lab had used up all but a microscopic amount of the blood sample he had recovered from the basement of the Reese house. So West had put the case file back.

"At [that] stage of DNA testing, the tiny bit that was left of the blood sample after the blood typing wasn't big enough for DNA testing," said Detective West.

West knew, however, that there was another sample of blood that could perhaps be analyzed for DNA. "There was blood on the large piece of carpeting I found . . . the carpeting I believe the Reeses had wrapped Dawn up in. The blood on this carpeting had been typed and found to be type O, and there was still a considerable amount of it left. In the 1990s, I filled out a request to have the FBI Laboratory examine the blood on the carpet and, if possible, do a DNA test on it. However, I would learn from the crime lab that the proteins in the blood sample from the carpet had degraded to the point it could not be tested for DNA." Smaller samples of blood are often stored in a freezer, but of course the carpet's size wouldn't allow this.

Naturally, West was greatly disappointed. He had hoped that the advent of DNA testing would move the case forward, but it hadn't.

"So again, the case stayed the way it was," said West. Still, the case and Paul Reese Sr. weighed on West's mind. He couldn't help but wonder what other crimes Paul Sr. may have been involved in that the police hadn't connected to him. "As I was getting ready to retire in 2007, I went back again to look through each of my remaining unsolved murder cases to request a DNA analysis and have it entered into the FBI's CODIS," said West. "From reviewing Dawn's case, I went back and obtained a buccal swab DNA sample from Paul Reese Sr. for a possible future comparison. Paul Reese Sr. seemed resigned to the fact and voluntarily gave me a cheek swab sample for comparison without any argument."

In late 2010, cold case detective Mark Albert was also thinking about the Reeses and the Dawn Marie Stuard case. He, too, wondered if, in light of the many scientific innovations and advances since 1986, there might be some new DNA evidence that could help move the case along. He telephoned the crime lab and was put in contact with a technician named Shelley Crispin. Albert told Crispin that he was looking into the Dawn Marie Stuard case and asked her to check and see if they still had any of the evidence left from the investigation.

"She said she would look for the evidence and see what she could do," said Detective Albert. "Between Thanksgiving and Christmas she was cleaning out the freezer at the crime lab and happened on to Dawn's blood sample way in the back, still there since 1986. She remembered me asking her about the case, and so she put it aside."

Upon talking with Crispin, Detective Albert found that DNA testing had, in the years since West's first request, progressed to the point where an analysis could be done even on microscopic amounts of evidence. The amount left after the blood typing in 1986, Crispin told him, met the requirements for analysis, and she assured him that a DNA test on the blood sample would be no problem. Detective Albert told Detective West about this—and while elated, West also knew that, in addition to the blood, other evidence would also need to be retested, specifically the carpet fibers found on Dawn and on the road close to where she had been dumped. They would need to be compared to the carpet fibers he had taken from the Reese house back in 1986.

Fortunately, the crime lab results from the new DNA testing on the blood came back just as Detective West had hoped they would. The blood he had recovered from the brick furnace flue in the Reese's basement in 1986 did indeed belong to Dawn Marie Stuard. Also, unlike in 1986, when the crime lab could only say that the carpet fibers found on Dawn's body were consistent with the fibers of the carpet samples taken from the Reese house, they were now able to state definitively that they were an exact match. Suddenly, this investigation now seemed very, very solvable.

"This was just the right time for the case," said Detective Mark Albert. "Everything just seemed to come together. I really feel like it was Roy's diligence in maintaining the case file, Shelley Crispin's attention to detail, and above all, Ted Stuard's plea for someone to come forward that were the key factors in bringing Dawn's case out of the cold case file."

Because of Detective Albert's efforts and the crime lab's results, Detective West now felt he had enough new evidence to reopen the case and have the murder charges refiled. He had wanted to do so desperately for years, and had even attempted it back in the 1990s only to have the Prosecutor's Office decline, but now, he was sure, was the time. West, retired from the Indianapolis Metropolitan Police Department and working for the Prosecutor's Office as an investigator for the grand jury, went to a senior member of the prosecutor's staff and presented his case.

"After I received the test results from the crime lab that said the blood from the furnace flue at the Reese house was Dawn Marie Stuard's, I went to Denise Robinson in the Prosecutor's Office," said West. "With these results and the other evidence it was decided that the best course was to file a murder charge against Paul

Reese Sr. Our strongest case was against him." He added, "We knew that he was the last person to see Dawn alive. Paul Reese Jr. had an alibi for the time of Dawn's murder, him being with Timothy Keller that day. He didn't get home until after 6:00 P.M., which the pathologist said was after Dawn had died."

Paul Reese Sr. had been the last person to be seen with Dawn, and his criminal record showed that he had a propensity for violence. He had served time in prison for trying to kill a girlfriend and had been released only a couple of years before the Dawn Marie Stuard murder. And although the police had also arrested the son, Paul Reese Jr., in 1986 for Dawn's murder, Paul Jr. had had witnesses who swore he'd been across town at the time of the murder, at the flea market with Timothy Keller. Since the murder involved a sexual assault, Robinson felt that they could additionally rule out the mother, Barbara Reese, as the murderer. And even though West had a witness who claimed to have seen Paul Jr. and Barbara help Paul Sr. carry the suspicious carpet roll out of the house, the statute of limitations had run out on prosecuting them for their involvement in the crime, so they couldn't be charged with helping to dispose of the body. Robinson also decided against refiling the rape charge due to the lack of semen as evidence. She felt much more confident that they would be able to convict Paul Reese Sr. on the murder charge.

"When I first reviewed the Paul Reese Sr. case I felt that prosecution of the case would be extremely difficult," said deputy prosecutor Denise Robinson. "There were multiple conflicting statements taken from witnesses which I felt the defense could exploit. Also, some of the witnesses, law enforcement and civilian, were now unavailable or had no recollection of that day or these events. On the other hand, the reexamination of the evidence, particularly for DNA, enhanced the strength of the case. Detective West and I met numerous times on the case to discuss the strengths and weaknesses, and ultimately I decided to take the chance and file the case."

Even with the reduced charges, Detective West felt as if a dark cloud that had been drifting around in his mind since 1986 suddenly dissipated. Perhaps at last Dawn Marie Stuard was going to receive some kind of justice. West also knew that Dawn's family would be elated by the refiling of the charges but would likely question why the Prosecutor's Office had only charged Paul Reese Sr. He tried as best he could to explain to them the realities of the situation.

"I know that Dawn's family would have liked us to charge Barbara Reese and Paul Reese Jr. with assisting in the crime," said West. "But the fact was that the statute of limitations simply wouldn't let us, and so they couldn't be charged."

Ted Stuard did feel disappointed that everyone involved in the crime wasn't going to be held responsible, but he was happy that the main participant was going to be prosecuted. And yet, along with feeling elated that the case was finally going to trial, he also couldn't help but feel that it was a shame that other people, specifically

Jason Fishburn, Clifford Haddix, Demetrius Allen, and Crystal Joy Jenkins, had had to be injured and killed in order to get his daughter's case revived.

"If Brian Reese hadn't gotten involved in that stupid stuff with his father, this case probably would never have been revived," said Ted Stuard. Ted also couldn't thank his wife enough for the part she had played in the re-opening of Dawn's case. "If it hadn't been for Linda this would still have been a closed case," said Ted Stuard. "She was the one who got it started up again. She's the one who called Detective Albert."

Linda Stuard, though, passed along the credit. "Detective Albert doesn't get enough praise for what he did," she said. "But he's the one who I believe really got the case started up again."

Of course, while Linda Stuard and Detective Mark Albert both played important parts, much of the credit belonged to Detective Sergeant Roy West. He had never forgotten about the Dawn Marie Stuard case, had looked at the case again and again, and had tried several times to get the Prosecutor's Office to refile the charges. Now, with the new evidence, all of his work was finally going to come to fruition at the trial of Paul Reese Sr. West could imagine with a smile the look of shock and surprise that would come to the elder Reese's face when the police arrested him again for Dawn's murder. Paul Reese Sr. had more than likely believed that he had gotten away with it.

A murder trial, however, requires a lot of preparation

and was months away, yet West still felt excited. He had had a long and lauded career as a homicide detective, but if he could just get a conviction in the Dawn Marie Stuard case, he felt his most poignant regret about his time in Homicide—his unsolved first murder case—would finally be erased.

FOURTEEN

On February 17, 2011, the Marion County Prosecutor's Office formally charged Paul Reese Sr. with the murder of Dawn Marie Stuard. "Over the years, Paul Reese Sr. was a suspect in the death of Dawn Marie Stuard, but dedicated police work and recent DNA evidence are what ultimately led to the charge filed today," Marion County prosecutor Terry Curry said in a press release. "Sergeant West took this case and never let go."

Getting the charge filed, however, was only the first step. Now West and deputy prosecutor Denise Robinson had to prepare the case for court. Getting a murder case ready for prosecution is an extremely involved process. Getting a murder case that is over a quarter century old ready for prosecution is even more difficult.

"An intense amount of preparation is needed in a homicide cold case like the Dawn Marie Stuard murder," said Robinson. "The prosecutor has to completely understand the twenty-six-year history of the case and every nuance of that history. I spent hours with Detective West discussing the case, and hours meeting with witnesses and the crime lab. I also went to the crime scene several times, as well as other areas relevant to the investigation."

"Any prosecutor who has tried murder cases will attest: there's no such thing as a 'simple homicide case,'" Johnson County, Indiana, prosecutor Lance Hamner said. "Witnesses must be meticulously interviewed, evidence must be protected both physically and legally, and arguments must be crafted so that they are as persuasive to the unsophisticated juror as to the highly educated one. The grueling process ends only when the verdict is read. And the verdict must be unanimous, or it's not a verdict at all."

Preparing a murder case for prosecution, besides planning a counterstrategy for whatever tactic the defense may be working up, also involves insuring that the original physical evidence is still available, that any new physical evidence that may have come to light is properly secured, that any new witnesses are thoroughly interviewed, that the original witnesses can be located, in this case after over a quarter century, and that these original witnesses are reinterviewed, if possible.

The reinterviews with the original witnesses in a homicide cold case, especially in a case like this when so much time has passed since the initial interviews, are very important. The detective and prosecutor must be certain that the testimony of the witnesses will be the same as in the original interviews. In a case like this, with so much time lapsing between the crime and the trial preparation, many things can happen to a witness's memory or motivation to talk, and when a prosecutor goes to trial, he or she doesn't want any surprises. A defense attorney will vigorously attack the credibility of any witness who seems to be telling a different story from the original one told to the police.

And adding even more complexity to this case, the prosecution knew that it had three witnesses who would be extremely vulnerable to character attacks by the defense. All three were convicted criminals, currently incarcerated. James L. Reese, Paul Reese Sr.'s older brother, had contacted the police back in 1986 and told them that his brother had admitted Dawn's rape and murder to him, and that he was willing to testify about it. However, in 2012 he sat in an Arizona prison, convicted of child molestation. An inmate at the Pendleton Correctional Facility named DeAngelo Gaines, who had shared a cell with Paul Reese Sr., had also contacted the police and said that Paul Sr. had confessed the crime to him, too. And in January 2011, an inmate at the Hendricks County Jail claimed that he had been present at the Reese house on March 17, 1986, and had overheard Paul Jr. arguing with his father. The inmate said he heard Paul Jr. ask his father, "Why did you have Mom do that, man?" The witness said that he later talked with Paul Jr., who told him that his mom had taken the carpet and dumped it along her paper route. These three witnesses had to be extensively interviewed to be certain their testimony would stand up under cross-examination.

And so, West went to work with the evidence and the new and old witnesses, giving the case the same meticulous attention he had given to every other murder case he'd had during his long career as a homicide detective. And again, this case was special to him. It had been his first case. It had involved a totally innocent victim. And it had gone unsolved. West deeply wanted this case solved and closed. He wanted to be standing there when Paul Reese Sr. received an appropriate and lengthy sentence.

Finally, after over a year of preparation, the prosecution felt it was ready to go to trial. On June 18, 2012, more than twenty-six years after the death of Dawn Marie Stuard, the trial for her murder finally began in Criminal Court 2 in Indianapolis, with Judge Robert Altice presiding. Michelle Wall, an attorney with the Public Defender's Office, represented Paul Reese Sr., who had been brought down to Indianapolis from the prison in Pendleton. Deputy prosecutors Denise Robinson and Mark Hollingsworth would handle the prosecution.

Before the trial began, Wall told the judge that she was concerned about the name Reese. She feared that prospective jurors would recognize it because of all the media attention Brian Reese had received, and would relate the name to the family's past criminal history. Judge Altice said he would ask all prospective jurors if they knew Mr. Reese or anything about him. Wall also said she was concerned about the State calling DeAngelo Gaines to testify because it would let the jurors know that Paul Reese Sr. had been incarcerated when he spoke with him. The judge said he would allow the testimony but instruct the jurors not to infer any criminal actions from Paul Sr. having been incarcerated. With these motions out of the way, the trial could begin.

The first step, of course, was jury selection. Good defense attorneys and prosecutors know that they can help their cases, no matter how tough they are, through careful jury selection. In this case (as opposed to Brian Reese's case, where his lawyer was merely hoping for a reduced sentence), the defense attorney needed jurors whom she could convince that Paul Reese Sr. was innocent of Dawn's murder. And, of course, the prosecutor, Denise Robinson, needed jurors whom she could convince that Paul Reese Sr. *was* guilty of Dawn's murder.

Still, the jury selection process in the Paul Reese Sr. case didn't take long. It began at 9:00 A.M. on June 18, 2012, and by 1:30 P.M. the prosecution and defense had agreed on seven women and five men.

Linda Stuard thought that the prosecution had done a good job with jury selection, with one exception. "There was a young man on the jury that I worried about," she said. "He didn't seem to be paying attention."

Following the seating of the jury at 1:30 P.M., the judge ordered a short recess. He scheduled opening statements to begin at 3:00 P.M.

In any serious criminal trial, the defense attorney naturally has the defendant clean up for court, even if his or her client is incarcerated, as was the case with Paul Reese Sr. Instead of wearing an orange prison jumpsuit, he showed up well groomed and in a shirt and tie. He paid close attention to the proceedings, leaning over every once in a while to confer with his attorney.

During her opening statement, deputy prosecutor Denise Robinson told the jury, "[Dawn] was brutalized, she was strangled, her body was dumped in a ravine." She also told them that they'd "hear a lot about carpeting and fibers at this trial." She then told the jury that she intended to show that the person responsible for Dawn's murder was Paul Reese Sr.

Defense attorney Michelle Wall, on the other hand, told the jury that it was impossible for the State to prove that Paul Reese Sr. had killed Dawn Marie Stuard. She said that she would show that there had been many people in and out of the house on Bosart Street that day, and that any one of them could have murdered Dawn.

The first person prosecutors called to testify the next day, June 19, 2012, was Officer Jeremiah Sedam, the first officer to respond to the crime scene. After being sworn in, he told the court that a dispatcher sent him to the 4600 block of East 23rd Street to secure the crime scene. He described the area to the court as consisting of a lot of trees and debris. Sedam said that he could see the body at the bottom of the hill, lying among the trash and debris, but that he didn't go down. He waited for Homicide. Sedam told the jurors that he was the first one at the crime scene, and that he secured it, and then made sure that no one entered the crime scene before Homicide got there. The defense had no cross-examination, so the judge excused him.

Following Officer Sedam, the prosecution put Kathleen Rueter on the witness stand. She described how she'd been out walking her daughter, who was then six years old, to school when she saw Dawn's body. School started at 1:00 P.M., so she estimated that she'd discovered the body at around 12:45 P.M. Again, the defense had no cross-examination, and the judge excused her.

The prosecution next put Ted Stuard, Dawn's father, on the stand. He told the jury about how he and his wife, Sandy, had frantically searched for their daughter on the night of March 16, 1986. He also related how he had felt strange while looking through the Reese house. "I was hoping I would find her, but I had a very bad feeling," he told the court. "It felt very eerie for some reason." He also said that the garage had no electricity and he didn't have a flashlight with him, so he really couldn't see much. Ted said that when he looked through the house, he called Dawn's name, but didn't open doors, boxes, closets, et cetera.

During his testimony, Ted Stuard looked constantly at Paul Reese Sr., and he later said that when he did, he could feel the anger building up inside him. "I felt cold-blooded rage when I saw Paul Reese Sr. in court," he said. "I just wanted to walk over and grab him by the throat and squeeze until he never breathed again."

Linda Stuard, who had accompanied her husband to court, added that after her husband's testimony, "He was so mad that he was squeezing my hand so hard I had to get it away from him."

Following Ted Stuard's testimony, the prosecution

then put on the witness stand a woman by the name of Lorrie Ann Hendrix. After being sworn in, she told the court that she had been best friends with Dawn Marie Stuard in 1986. Lorrie said that she had been the one who introduced Dawn to Johnny and Jeremy Reese. They both thought the two boys were cute. She said she liked Jeremy and Dawn liked Johnny, so they started hanging out with them (before they were confined at the Juvenile Detention Facility). Lorrie added that Dawn was supposed to come by her house the weekend she died, but that she hadn't shown up.

Next up was Detective Roy West. This would be the first of several times he took the stand over the course of the trial. West gave the court a complete rundown of everything he had seen and done at the crime scene. He said he'd called for the Crime Lab while en route to the scene, and that he'd arrived there at 1:56 P.M. He also told about talking with the detective who'd been in charge of Dawn's runaway case, and learning from him, along with the Stuards, about the Reeses.

When the prosecutor finished with West, the defense then had an opportunity to cross-examine him, but defense attorney Michelle Wall declined to do so at this point. While many defense attorneys hope to be able to get witnesses for the prosecution to contradict themselves on the stand, and then attack their credibility when they do so, Detective West was much too seasoned an officer for that to happen. West, having testified in hundreds of cases, was a very sincere and believable witness whom the defense attorney likely couldn't shake. He simply hadn't given the defense attorney anything to grab onto.

The State's next witness called to testify would be Officer Edwin Andresen. Andresen had been the evidence technician West had used for this investigation. After being sworn in, Andresen told the court that he received the run at 1:56 P.M. He described the crime scene as wooded and littered with debris. The prosecutor then played a video Andresen had made of the crime scene and had him narrate what the jurors were seeing, including the body. The State next introduced a number of crime scene photographs and had Andresen identify them. Andresen then went over the various pieces of evidence he had collected that day, including the carpet pieces and fibers found at the scene. Also, he told about photographing a footprint at the crime scene. It appeared that someone had slipped on the steep slope. The defense again had no cross-examination, so the judge excused him.

Following Officer Andresen, the State recalled Detective Roy West to the witness stand. He told the court that the body had been located far enough away from the road that he believed it wasn't just tossed out of a car, but rather carried down to the dump site. West also pointed out that mud and dirt on the back of Dawn's clothing indicated she had been dragged. He then told the jurors about having all the individuals at the house on Bosart Street taken down to police headquarters for questioning, and that he'd also sent a car to pick up Paul Sr. at

Crawford's Tavern when he found out that Paul Sr. had been calling the house on Bosart Street from there. West next talked about serving the search warrant at 1428 North Bosart Street, and how he began his search at 6:30 P.M. on March 22, 1986, and ended at 5:10 A.M. the next morning. He also mentioned that he had had the Reese's station wagon towed to a secure location for processing.

On March 24, 1986, West told the court, he obtained a search warrant for the body of Paul Reese Sr. During this, he had a blood sample taken. He also talked about searching the area around East 19th Street and North Forest Manor Avenue, where he recovered the large piece of carpeting that had been dumped near some trees.

When West finished, the defense again declined to cross-examine.

Prosecutors then recalled Officer Edwin Andresen to the witness stand. They had him identify photographs he had taken at 1428 North Bosart Street of both the house and the vehicles parked there. He next identified the pieces of carpeting he had recovered on the ground outside of the Reese house, and identified the pictures he had taken of the interior of the Reese garage and the pieces of carpeting recovered there. He then told the court about finding a roll of duct tape in a cabinet in the garage, and of photographing the brick furnace flue where he recovered the blood sample.

Following this testimony, Andresen then said that he had found green and gold carpeting in the Reese basement, outside the Reese house, and in their garage similar to that at the crime scene. In a wastebasket in the basement he also found pieces of newspaper with spray paint on them. Next, he talked about recovering a photo album from the basement that contained newspaper articles about Dawn Marie Stuard's murder. After this, Andresen spoke about processing the brown 1976 Pontiac Le Mans Safari station wagon belonging to the Reeses. He said that the rear compartment, unlike the rest of the car, was uncluttered, as if it had recently carried something. Every other area of the car, he said, was filled with trash. With Detective West's search warrant for the person of Paul Reese Sr., he told the jurors he collected a pair of jeans, a brown leather belt, a dress shirt, one blue and white handkerchief, black socks, white underwear, two tubes of blood, pubic hair samples, head hair samples, and fingernail scrapings. He then told them that he had also collected copies of the *Indianapolis Star* newspaper for the same dates as those found at the crime scene and at the Reese house. These would be used for comparison if needed.

Defense attorney Michelle Wall did decide to cross-examine this time. She asked Andresen who had lived in the basement where the photo albums with the articles about Dawn's murder had been found. He told her he didn't know.

After Officer Andresen finished with his testimony and the judge excused him, the prosecution and defense stipulated approval on the chain of custody for items recovered during Dawn's autopsy, which included blood samples, vaginal and anal slides, fibers from her clothing, hair samples, fingernail scrapings, and Dawn's clothing. Most important for the prosecution, of course, were Dawn's blood samples, so that they could be compared to the blood taken from the brick furnace flue.

Next up the prosecution called Dr. Dean Hawley to testify. He told the court that he was currently a forensic pathologist at the Indiana University School of Medicine. In March 1986, however, he had been a new doctor and worked at the Coroner's Office as a deputy coroner. He told the court about responding to the Dawn Marie Stuard crime scene.

He said, "The biggest question was whether the victim had died there or elsewhere."

Dr. Hawley then went on to tell the jurors that he believed the victim had been killed elsewhere and then moved to the area on 23rd Street because the victim had suffered postmortem wounds from being dragged and dumped there. Dawn's body, he said, had scrape marks on her back with dirt but no blood in them. He told the jurors how, contrary to television and movies, an exact time of death can't always be determined, and he estimated that she had been there at least twelve hours.

Dr. Hawley had also assisted Dr. Gauger at the autopsy, so he was able to tell the court about it as well. He said that Dawn's fingernails had been so short that they could only get very small scrapings from them. She had sustained a large bruise on the bridge of her nose, and also contusions on her forehead, right eye, and right cheek. He said that under her scalp on the back of her head they found quite a bit of bleeding. Further examination of Dawn's body found tape adhesive on her mouth and wrists (some of the skin on her left wrist had been peeled off when someone removed the tape before dumping the body). He said that tests in 1986 showed that this adhesive came from duct tape. They also found carpet fibers on her clothing, on her body, and in her mouth.

He went on to say that the injury to the left side of the back of Dawn's head looked as though she had violently struck something, and that the brick furnace flue fit the bill nicely. He told the court, "Because of the force required to produce the internal damage under the scalp and in the brain, [the brick flue] would have been an ideal surface contact for the injury to the left side of the back of the head." Dr. Hawley thought the blow had likely caused unconsciousness. He told the jurors that during their examination of Dawn's body, they had found petechiae—burst blood vessels usually caused by strangulation—on her face along with fingernail marks where she had fought to stop the strangulation, digging her fingernails into her skin as she tried to push away the object strangling her. The doctor believed that it had probably taken her murderer three to four minutes to kill Dawn.

Talking about the injury to her throat, Dr. Hawley said that the wound pattern was not that of a rope or cord, but of a straight hard object. He added that a pool cue taken from the Reese house "bears an enormous resemblance to an object that would create the surface abrasion [on Dawn's throat] and could also create the internal injury, could create the asphyxiation, and the brain damage."

He also told the jurors that Dawn had injuries to both her vagina and anus caused by forcible sexual contact, which included abrasions, lacerations, and tearing of the tissue. All of this, he said, had occurred prior to her death.

Prosecutor Denise Robinson then interjected, "So she was brutalized before she died?" The defense attorney immediately objected to the word "brutalized." Judge Altice sustained the objection and told the jurors to disregard it.

During her cross-examination, defense attorney Michelle Wall asked Dr. Hawley if the injury to the back of Dawn's head had likely caused unconsciousness. He answered yes. She then asked what he thought had happened. He said, "Someone slammed her head into the bricks with the pool cue across the front of her throat." Wall then asked if the injuries to Dawn's vagina and anus could have come from consensual sex. Dr. Hawley said yes, they could have.

Next the prosecution called Valerie Ladner to the witness stand. After being sworn in, Ladner said that she had been a forensic serologist at the Crime Lab in Indianapolis in 1986. She told the court that she had received the blood sample taken from the brick furnace flue. She typed it and found that it was blood type O. Ladner told the jurors that she next examined the oral, vaginal, and rectal slides taken from Dawn, but found no semen. Nor had she found any semen in Dawn's underwear, or any blood on the pool cues that had been submitted for examination. When she finished testifying, the defense declined to cross-examine, and the judge excused her.

The next witness called by the prosecution to testify was Barbara Crim-Swanson. She told the court that she worked as a forensic scientist at the Kansas Bureau of Investigation Forensic Laboratory and was the casework supervisor for the biology DNA section. Crim-Swanson stated that she had been employed by the Crime Lab in Indianapolis from 1987 to 1996. She then explained to the jurors that when DNA analysis first came into use, they had required a large sample, relatively free of environmental contamination, in order to test it. She went on to say that in 1987 she tested the fingernail scrapings from Dawn. Under one of Dawn's left fingernails, Crim-Swanson had found the presence of blood, but the sample had been too small to test. She added that she'd also found blood on the large piece of carpeting Detective West had recovered from East 19th Street and North Forest Manor Avenue. She'd examined it and found it to be type O. Crim-Swanson then added that she found indications of human blood on the carpeting taken from the basement of the Reese house, but that the sample had not been large enough for further testing.

The defense had no cross-examination. Following this, the court recessed for the day.

FIFTEEN

The next morning, June 20, 2012, when testimony in the trial of Paul Reese Sr. for the murder of Dawn Marie Stuard in 1986 resumed, the prosecution once more called Detective Roy West to the witness stand. He told the court that Mrs. Carol Luken, the neighbor who had witnessed the Reeses carrying the roll of sagging carpet out of their house early in the morning, eventually told a coworker of hers about what she had seen. She had felt guilty about not telling the officers who came to her house the day following Dawn's disappearance about what she had seen, and she figured her coworker friend, who was a deputy sheriff, would know what to do with the information. The deputy sheriff had immediately contacted Roy West, who then went to see Carol Luken. Although she hadn't told the detectives about what she'd seen during their canvass on March 17, 1986, in November 1987 she told Detective West the complete story.

The prosecution then called Timothy Joe Keller to testify. He started by telling the court that he was now married with five kids and made his living junking cars and going to flea markets. He said he had been close friends with Paul Reese Jr. in 1986, and that he'd called Paul Sr. "Big Paul" and Paul Jr. "Little Paul." When asked where he lived in 1986, he said that he lived sometimes with his grandmother and sometimes with a girlfriend named Carol Wampler. He told the court that he had seen Dawn Stuard quite a few times at the Reese house.

When asked why Dawn came to the Reese house so often, he said, "She did a paper route with Barbara Reese and she was over there all the time because, you know, they were all just friends."

The prosecutor then moved on to where Timothy and Paul Jr. had gotten the items they were going to try to sell at the Liberty Bell Flea Market on March 16, 1986. Timothy said Paul Jr. had stolen a pink bicycle and a lawn mower that had been sitting out. They had "helped themselves" to these items, he admitted.

The questioning next moved on to the day that Dawn was killed. Timothy said that on March 16, 1986, Dawn had arrived about fifteen minutes after he did. "She came in and wanted to play pool with Paul Sr.," he told the court. "She had come over because she was wanting to go on the paper route with Barbara [to collect payment]."

He added that when he returned to the Reese house after going to pick up some items to sell at the flea market, he saw Dawn standing in the kitchen with Paul Sr.

Apparently, some part of his earlier statements to the police didn't match exactly what he had just said in court, and the prosecutor asked him to read his earlier statement. Timothy told the court that he had quit school and couldn't read, so the court reporter read it out loud for him. Timothy then corrected his earlier testimony and said that after he and Paul Jr. came back to the house, Dawn let them in and that she had a pool cue in her hand. Paul Sr. had not been upstairs when they came back.

Timothy told the court that he and Paul Jr. were at the flea market until around 4:30 or 5:00 P.M. He stated that Paul Jr. only left his sight once, for about thirty minutes. A round trip to the Bosart Street address would have taken well over an hour. Next, he added, on the night of March 16, 1986, right after they got back from the flea market, Paul Jr. borrowed his white Pinto. "He said he was going on a date with Dawn Stuard, or something," Timothy said. "I don't remember for certain, but I'm pretty sure that's what it was."

Paul Jr. returned the car to Timothy at about 8:00 P.M. "He drove it a little funny and it had mud on it," Timothy told the jurors. "The backseat was down, there was a little tape in the back of it all balled up, and my speakers were moved. Also a pool cue was in the back, a half of one, the top half. There were also some newspapers in it with spray paint on them." Timothy said he threw everything away because he thought it was trash.

Immediately after this, Timothy went on, Paul Sr. said he needed a ride. "He said he wanted to go look at some tires."

The prosecutor then showed Timothy the photograph of a road. "Do you recognize that road?"

"Uh, yes," Timothy answered.

"What road does that appear to you to be?"

"It was the road where Dawn's body was found."

"Is that the road that Paul Sr. told you to drive to?"

"Yes."

The questioning then moved on to Paul Sr.'s supposed reason for wanting to drive on that road. Timothy said that Paul Sr. told him that he wanted to look for tires, and that they drove over to a truck full of tires. The prosecutor asked if Paul Sr. went up and talked to anyone about the tires.

"No. Either they was for sale, or he was—or he was going to steal them."

"Did Paul Reese Sr. ask you to drive anywhere else?" the prosecutor asked.

"Yeah, a little ball stadium off of 21st [Street]."

"Why did he want to go there?"

"I don't really know. I don't know why we went over there."

Timothy said that when he and Paul Sr. returned to the house on Bosart Street they saw a brown truck parked out in front. Paul Sr. had Timothy drop him off down the street. Following this, Timothy drove to his girl-friend's apartment, and during the drive he saw someone following him. He didn't know who it was but believed it was someone from Dawn's family. It was Wesley, and he came to the apartment and asked Timothy if he had seen Dawn or knew where she was. Timothy told him no, but said that he came back several more times and asked him the same question. The police also visited Timothy that night and questioned him about the pink bicycle that Paul Jr. had stolen and tried to sell at the flea market. The officers towed Timothy's white Pinto away and came inside his girlfriend's apartment and looked around.

He then added that Ted Stuard also showed up that night and asked him if he knew anything about Dawn. Timothy said he took Ted to Doyle Stinson's house to see if he knew anything. They also drove over to the Reese house. "We knocked on the door," Timothy told the court, "and he asked questions about Dawn, asking them if they had seen her or not."

The prosecution turned the witness over to the defense for cross-examination. Michelle Wall asked Timothy Keller if it was true that he had given five statements to the police. Timothy said yes.

"Is it fair in characterizing," Wall asked, "that there was a lot you testified to today that you did not tell Detective West at that time [1986]?"

"Yes."

Wall, perhaps trying to establish some guilt on Paul Jr., asked Timothy how he would describe the way Paul Jr. had looked when he'd returned the Pinto that night.

"A little upset, maybe a little—I mean, not like he was when he picked up the car. His hair was a little messed up, his face kind of red. Seemed a little grouchy."

"And the last time you saw Dawn was when she was coming up in the morning with the pool cue in hand. You would say that there were a lot of people there—in and out of the house, that you didn't see her again, but that she could have been there, along with lots of other people. Is that right?"

"Yeah," Timothy answered. "I mean, I don't know."

The cross-examination finished, and the prosecution asked one question on redirect, which was whether Timothy still associated with the Reeses. He answered, "No, not for many years, no."

Once the judge had excused him and Timothy Keller left the stand, the prosecution called Dawn's cousin Wesley Collins to testify. When asked about Dawn and the day of March 16, 1986, he responded, "Usually she was down there [at our house] by no later than 3:00 P.M. in the afternoon. She usually had chores to take care of in the morning and stuff, and would take care of that and then she would head down to the house by that afternoon."

The prosecutor then asked what he did when Dawn hadn't shown up that Sunday.

"I went over to the Village Pantry because she sometimes [walked] over there to get something to drink. I drove around the neighborhood a bit. It was around four in the afternoon." He added that at 5:00 he went back to Dawn's house, but she wasn't there. Then he talked to a neighbor across the street who said he had seen Dawn the previous night with the newspaper lady, who Wesley knew was Barbara Reese. And so, he drove his car over to the Reese house on Bosart Street. The two Reese girls, he found, were playing out front. He asked the two girls if they had seen Dawn, and they told him, yes, she had been there earlier. At that point Barbara Reese came to the door and told him that she hadn't seen Dawn, but that she had been there earlier but had left.

Following this, Wesley told the jurors, he returned home to see if anyone there had heard anything about Dawn. It was then 6:15 P.M. He stayed at home a bit, but then returned to the Reese house at around 7:00 P.M. One of the Reese daughters answered the door and he spoke with her and to Barbara again, but he got the same responses. He then left the Reese house and went back to Dawn's house to get a photograph of his cousin to show Barbara Reese. He wanted to be certain that she knew who he was talking about. Barbara had seemed to him to be very evasive about Dawn. And so, he took the photograph back to the Reese house and asked for Barbara, showing her the picture. She assured him that she knew who Dawn was and that the last person to see her had been Paul Reese Sr., but that he had left, and she didn't know where he had gone.

Wesley left the Reese house and again returned to Dawn's house, just in case she might have shown up, and then returned to his own house. He told the court that he was pretty upset by then because he had been looking for Dawn for four to five hours without finding any sign of her.

A little while later, Wesley said, he returned once again to the Reese house to see if Paul Sr. had shown up there yet. He hadn't, so Wesley sat in his car a few houses down from the Reese house and watched the residence, waiting for Paul Sr. to return. He told the jurors that he sat there for ten or fifteen minutes until he saw a white Ford Pinto pull up in front of the Reese house. Someone got out of the car, but he couldn't see who it was. The Pinto then took off at a high rate of speed, and Wesley followed it to the Glen Ridge Apartments. The driver of the Pinto got out and headed for one of the apartments. Wesley followed him and found that it was Timothy Keller. Wesley said he knocked on the apartment door Keller had gone into. A girl answered and he asked for Keller, who came to the door. When Wesley asked Keller if he knew anything about Dawn and if he had just dropped off Paul Sr., Keller said that he didn't know anything about Dawn, and that, yes, he had just dropped off Paul Sr. at the house on Bosart Street.

Wesley drove straight back to the Reese house and told Barbara that he wanted to talk to Paul Sr. But Barbara insisted that Paul Sr. wasn't there. Following this, Wesley once more checked Dawn's house and then returned home. He didn't stay long, though, because he drove back over to the apartment where Keller was staying and asked him if he had really dropped off Paul Sr. at the house on Bosart Street. Keller assured him that he had dropped off Paul Sr.

Not knowing what else to do, Wesley drove home and told his mother everything that had happened. He then returned and sat in his car down the street from the Reese house. He told the court that he never saw or talked with Paul Sr. that night. While Wesley sat in the car, he said his mother was calling Dawn's friends and checking hangouts she might have gone to. Ted and Sandy, he said, showed up a little after 10:00 P.M., and that he returned to the Reese house that night with Ted. Following this, he drove around looking for Dawn until well after midnight.

The prosecution then turned the witness over to the defense for cross-examination. Defense attorney Michelle Wall asked Wesley if he was positive about the times, and if he and his family knew that Dawn had hung around with the Reeses. He said, yes, he was pretty certain of the times, and that Dawn's parents would never have allowed her to hang around with the Reeses. He said there was no way they had known she'd been spending time there.

The next witness the prosecution called to testify was Wesley's wife, Michelle Collins. After being sworn in, she told the court that her name in 1986 had been Michelle Lynch, that she had been Wesley's girlfriend then, and had lived with him and his mother, Mona. She told the court that Wesley had had a 1980 yellow Mercury Zephyr in 1986 and that she had driven around in it with him while he was looking for Dawn. She also said that she accompanied Wesley and Ted when they went to the Reese house.

The prosecutor then asked her, "When asking questions of Mrs. Reese . . . about Dawn's whereabouts, did one of the girls say something?"

"She did," Michelle answered.

"And did you see Mrs. Reese do anything when one of the girls started to say something?"

"She slapped her across the face."

"And did that end whatever it was the little girl was going to say?"

"Yes, it sure did."

Michelle then told the jurors how, while trying to figure out what to do, she had rummaged through Dawn's belongings and found several pieces of paper with telephone numbers on them. She then started calling these numbers, but nothing came of it. She also said that she was at the Reese house when a couple of police officers, investigating the runaway report, showed up there. The prosecutor thanked her and turned Michelle over to the defense.

The defense had only one question on cross-examination. Michelle was asked what time the search for Dawn started. She responded that it started around 5:00 to 5:30 P.M.

Officer James Jarrett, the next witness for the prosecution, then took the witness stand. He said that in 1986 he had been assigned to a patrol district close to the Reese house.

"I was given a radio run through IPD dispatch," he told the court, "to go to the residence of the Reese family to investigate a runaway report on Dawn Stuard." He added that when he began talking to Barbara Reese that night outside her house, explaining why he was there,

"Mrs. Reese then interrupted what I was saying, became very animated, very excited, just talking very fast."

"Did you get any information that assisted you in locating Dawn Stuard?" the prosecutor asked.

"No."

The defense, once the prosecution had finished, said it had no questions for cross-examination.

The next witness, Officer Al Watson, said that in 1986 he was also assigned to a district close to the Reese household. On the night of March 16, 1986, he stated, he was investigating the theft of a pink girl's bicycle. He said the complainant had told the police that the bicycle had been stolen just a little after midnight on the morning of March 16, 1986, and that the thieves had driven away in a white Ford Pinto. The Reeses being the usual suspects, Officer Watson's investigation took him to the Reese house late in the evening of March 16. Barbara let him come in and allowed him to look around for the pink bicycle. He said he checked the basement and saw several bicycles there, but no pink one. He left and went to Timothy Keller's grandmother's house, where he located the white Ford Pinto. His witness, he told the court, came there and positively identified it as the car the thieves had been in. Officer Watson said he then looked inside the white Pinto and found the pink bicycle that Keller and Paul Jr. apparently hadn't been able to sell that day at the flea market, as well as a tree stand that had also been reported stolen. He had the Pinto impounded at 11:44 P.M. Officer Watson said he then returned to the Reese house to assist Officer Jarrett in his investigation of the runaway report. Neither of them, he added, saw or spoke with Paul Sr. that night.

The cross-examination by the defense consisted only of verifying the times of the events.

Following Officer Watson's testimony, Doyle Dean Stinson took the witness stand. Upon being sworn in, he told the jurors that in 1986 he had been friends with one of the other Reese boys, Johnny. When asked, Doyle said that he had seen Dawn Stuard once out collecting payment with Barbara on her paper route. He then told about how, on March 16, 1986, he went to the back door of the Reese house. Dawn answered the door and he'd asked if Johnny was there, apparently unaware he was confined at the Juvenile Detention Facility.

"I thought I heard a scuffle," Doyle said. "I didn't see her arm move. Somebody slammed that door. I don't see how that was able, but that's what happened. The way it looked was that somebody was behind the door."

The defense attorney, upon cross-examination, asked why Doyle had gone to the Reese house that day, and he said that it was because he needed a ride to go sell a motorcycle. Michelle Wall then asked if Dawn Stuard had seemed upset when she answered the door, and Stinson said no, she hadn't.

Archie Ward, a neighbor of the Reeses in 1986, next took the witness stand. He said that he saw Dawn Stuard over at the Reese house several times, just hanging out and playing pool. He added that on the night of March 16, 1986, at around 5:30 P.M., he and a girlfriend went over to the Reese house. Paul Sr., Barbara, Pam Winningham (Paul Jr.'s live-in girlfriend), and one of the Reese daughters were there. Archie said that he and his girlfriend stayed for about ten to fifteen minutes.

The prosecutor then asked if he saw Paul Sr. later that night, and Archie answered that at around 10:30 to 11:00 Paul Sr. knocked on the door of his house at 4506 East 18th Street. He said that Paul Sr. had never been there before. His brother Jay answered the door, and he went with him.

When asked why Paul Sr. had come there, Archie answered, "Yeah, he was nervous, said that somebody was chasing him because of Dawn Stuard. He said they thought that he might have kidnapped her."

Archie continued by saying that Paul Sr. asked his mother for a ride, but she said no. He then asked to borrow a bicycle. Paul Sr. told them that he had stopped by Timothy Keller's place first, but that there were cops everywhere, and that they were searching Keller's car. Right about then, Archie said, he heard sirens in the neighborhood. Paul Sr. quickly pedaled away on the bicycle.

Upon cross-examination, the defense attorney asked about the people whom Archie had seen at the Reese house the night of March 16, and whether there could have been other people in the house whom he hadn't seen. Archie said it was possible. The defense then asked if he had earlier given a statement to the police that Paul Sr. had returned the bicycle twenty minutes after borrowing it. He said he didn't remember that.

Jay Ward followed his brother Archie to the witness

stand. He, too, said that he had seen Dawn at the Reese house several times, and he also told about Paul Sr. coming to his house on the night of March 16, and how he had never been there before.

When the prosecution asked about Paul Sr.'s demeanor that night, Jay answered, "Very nervous, because normally he never showed much emotion. He was very calm, just straight-faced most of the time. But this day he didn't; he seemed very nervous, unlike I'd ever seen him."

The prosecutor then asked why Paul Sr. had come over to the Wards' house. "The Stuard family was there [at the house on Bosart Street]," Jay said. "I guess they were chasing him. That's what he was saying. He was scared, so he wanted to get out of the neighborhood."

The next question the prosecution asked Jay Ward was what time Paul Reese returned to his house. "He did come back about fifteen or twenty minutes later," Jay answered. "He was in our backyard. He knocked on the back door, but my mother wouldn't let us open the door. I think she sensed something."

Following this, the prosecution asked if Jay had gotten a telephone call from Paul Sr. on March 17, 1986. "Yes," Jay said. "He called that Monday, wanting to know if the cops were still at his house, and if I would go down to his house and check and see if they were still there. He said he was calling from a bar." Jay told the court that he didn't go down to the house.

Upon cross-examination, the defense asked if Paul Sr. had said he just wanted to get out of the neighborhood, and not the state. Jay answered the neighborhood.

The next witness called to testify by the prosecution identified himself as Roger G. Glover, a retired Indianapolis police officer. He told the court that in the afternoon of March 17, 1986, he had been sent to Crawford's Tavern in the 1100 block of South Meridian Street. He and another officer went there to look for Paul Reese Sr.

The defense had no cross-examination questions.

Next up, William Decker also identified himself as a retired Indianapolis police officer. On March 17, 1986, he said, he went with Officer Glover to Crawford's Tavern. Also with them, he added, were two homicide detectives who had a picture of Paul Sr. Decker told the court that he walked up to the bar and asked Paul Sr. his name. He told Officer Decker that his name was Jerry Boyd but later admitted that he was Paul Reese Sr. The officers took him down to police headquarters for questioning by Detective West.

The defense again had no cross-examination questions.

The prosecution then called Pam Winningham to testify. In March 1986, Pam had been Paul Jr.'s girlfriend and had lived with him in the basement. When asked, Pam said she had seen Dawn a couple of times at the Reese house. She told the court that when she came up from the basement on the morning of March 16, 1986, she'd seen Dawn Stuard, Timothy Keller, and Paul Sr. all sitting in the kitchen. Dawn asked her if she wanted to play a game of pool, but Pam told her she couldn't. She had to leave with Paul Jr. and Timothy. She said that she saw several lawn mowers sitting in the back of Timothy's

Pinto, and that they returned to the Reese house because they had forgotten something they were going to take to the flea market. She then told the court about finding her father waiting for her out in front of the Reese house.

"When you got into the car with your father," the prosecutor asked, "did the two of you have an argument?"

"Yes, he smacked me," she answered. "I stayed at my Dad's house until about 4:30 P.M., then went back to the Reese house."

"When you got back to the Reese house, who did you see there?"

"Paul Sr."

"Anyone else?"

"No."

"Did you notice anything about his person that indicated what he had been doing just before you got there?" the prosecution asked.

"It looked like he had just got out of the shower."

"Did you see Dawn Stuard there?"

"No."

Pam went on to say that when she got back to the Reese house Paul Sr. told her not to go down into the basement because Paul Jr. was down there with another girl. Pam said she went right down there, but that no one was in the basement. The prosecution next asked how Paul Sr. had acted once she had returned to the Reese house.

"Kind of nervous," Pam answered. "He'd sit down and then he'd get up and walk to the window, then sit back down, then back up."

Pam then added that she and Paul Jr. went to bed at around 11:30 P.M. on March 16, 1986, but that she was awakened an hour or so later by a noise in the basement. "I asked who was there and Barbara said it was just her doing some laundry, but the washer and dryer weren't going." She said she also heard Paul Jr. talking to someone, but that she couldn't make out what he was saying. That was when she'd realized that he wasn't in bed with her.

The next afternoon, Pam went on, the police showed up at 1428 North Bosart Street. She drove up to the house with Paul Sr. in the car. Because the police were there, he wouldn't get out, but had her drive up the street a bit. He told her to call him at the Woodcutter's Bar when she found out why the police were there. Pam told the court that she didn't call him.

The defense attorney, upon cross-examination, asked Pam why she didn't say anything to the police in her statement about Paul Sr. telling her not to go down into the basement. She said she hadn't thought it was relevant at the time. The defense also asked if the washer and dryer even worked. Pam wasn't certain.

This ended the testimony for the day, and the judge admonished the jurors not to talk to anyone about the case.

On June 21, 2012, the prosecution began the day by bringing Carol Luken to the witness stand. After the bailiff had sworn her in, she told the court that in

1986 she'd lived on Nolan Avenue, which ran alongside the Reese house. From her home she'd had a clear view of the rear of the Reese house, which sat about seventy-five feet away. She said that she had seen Dawn Stuard at the Reese house several times.

The prosecution asked if there was some reason she had been up at around 1:00 A.M. on March 17, 1986.

"My dog had puppies and she wouldn't take care of them," Carol Luken told the jurors. "So I was up most of the night trying to keep the puppies alive."

"Was the area around your house and the Reeses' lighted?" the prosecution asked.

"There were two streetlights nearby."

The prosecution then asked Carol to tell the court about the events of that morning.

She told them that she looked out her kitchen window and, "I seen them [the Reeses] take the green car and shove it out into the street. The only reason I know this is because it was very loud." She said she also heard "loud talking, just real loud, and banging doors and stuff."

The prosecution asked what happened next. "They were pushing the car out onto the street," she went on, "the two boys were. And then one of them backed up the brown station wagon." She said she recognized one of the boys as Paul Jr. but couldn't tell who the other boy was.

When asked what they did with the brown station wagon, she answered, "It was backed up to the back door. All I seen was that they carried out a rolled-up rug and put it in the back of the station wagon."

The prosecutor asked who "they" were, and Carol said, "That would have been Paul Reese Jr. and Paul Reese Sr."

"Did you notice anything in particular about the rug?" the prosecutor asked.

"Yes, it sagged in the middle."

Carol Luken said that Barbara Reese opened the tailgate and drove the station wagon away with the headlights out. She also said that a lighter colored car followed behind the station wagon.

When asked why she had waited so long to report what she had witnessed, Carol said that she was frightened of the Reese family. However, she added, she felt guilty about not telling what had happened, so she eventually told a coworker about it, who then contacted Detective West. She said she suspected that her coworker would tell the proper people, because he was a reserve deputy sheriff.

The defense, during cross-examination, went over her testimony again but didn't uncover anything new.

When Carol Luken stepped down, Detective Sergeant Roy West once more took the witness stand and was asked what had happened to the Dawn Marie Stuard case after the prosecution closed it in 1987.

"I would continue to look at the case during my other investigations," he said, "to see if there were any additional people to talk to. A few times information would come in during those years. I would follow that information up, but nothing resulted from it." Two of these tips, he said, came from Crime Stoppers and named two specific men as suspects. However, West said, after he interviewed the men and checked out their stories, he eventually dropped both of them as suspects.

West then went on to tell the jurors about receiving a letter that a man named DeAngelo Gaines had sent to the police department. It had been postmarked December 17, 2010. In the letter Gaines claimed that Paul Reese Sr. had confessed Dawn's murder to him and that he was willing to testify in court about it. West interviewed Gaines on January 6, 2011. The prosecution then asked West if Gaines had been offered anything in return for his testimony. He said no.

DeAngelo Gaines then took the witness stand. He wore what appeared to be a small helmet. The prosecutor asked him about that and Gaines said it was to protect his head because he had epilepsy and grand mal seizures. He then told the jurors that he had been in the Marion County Jail, cell block 4D, on a burglary charge. The jailers put Paul Reese Sr. in the cell next to him, and they talked. "He told me he did something, that he was paying for something that was unrelated to what he was in for now. He said that he deserved it because he took someone's life. He said it happened over a quarter century before. It was a person who lived in the neighborhood."

Gaines went on to say that he ran into Paul Reese Sr. about four months later in the Pendleton Correctional Facility cafeteria, and that he was frightened because he had already written the letter and didn't know if Paul Sr. knew about it. When they spoke in the cafeteria, Gaines found that Paul Sr.'s attitude had changed since they'd talked in the Marion County Jail.

"He told me that he couldn't be convicted," Gaines told the jurors, "that the statute of limitations had run out on the crime. He told me that he could tell the President about it, and they couldn't do anything. He also told me that it was a young girl who was a friend of his youngest son, but that she had just stayed too late." Then, Gaines added, they had talked again later and Paul Sr. told him that he had hidden the body up near 21st or 26th Street.

The defense attorney, on cross-examination, asked if Gaines was having memory problems because of his seizures. Gaines replied not about Paul Reese Sr. Wall then tried to get Gaines to say that he had written the letter to the police in the hope that it would help with a post-conviction relief request he had submitted, but he said that that process was already over by the time he wrote the letter. He told the court that the judge in the case had already told him that since he had pleaded guilty, he had no grounds for an appeal. The defense attorney continued with a lengthy cross-examination in an attempt to get Gaines to say that he had written the letter because he hoped to get something in return, but she couldn't get him to.

"He wants you to believe that after one day of knowing him, [Paul Reese Sr.] told him all of his deepest, darkest secrets," defense attorney Michelle Wall would later tell the jury. "It makes no sense. They didn't even know each other. You cannot believe anything he says."

Still, when Wall asked DeAngelo Gaines if the state had offered him a reduced sentence for his testimony, he answered, "No, they haven't. They wouldn't even buy me lunch." This brought a laugh from the courtroom. There was then considerable recross and redirect questioning, but Gaines never wavered from his statement that he didn't expect, nor did he receive, anything for his testimony. The judge, seeing that the prosecution and the defense had no more questions, excused the witness.

Following DeAngelo Gaines's testimony, the prosecution asked that some stipulations the defense had agreed to be read into the record, specifically that the keeper of the records at the Marion County Jail confirmed that DeAngelo Gaines and Paul Reese Sr. had been in adjoining cells in cell block 4 at the same time. Also, the keeper of the records for the Pendleton Correctional Facility confirmed that Gaines and Paul Sr. had been there together in early 2011.

The prosecution next called Robert McCurdy to the witness stand. He told the court that he was a Ph.D. who worked for the Marion County Crime Lab. He said that he had examined the paint on the newspapers West had collected in 1986, both at the crime scene and from the Reese house, and found that they had a common origin.

The defense had no cross-examination.

Next, the prosecution had another stipulation read into the record. The stipulation said that John Mann of the Marion County Crime Lab had in 1986 examined the carpet samples taken from Dawn's body, from the Reese house, and from East 19th Street and North Forest Manor Avenue. He said at the time that they may all have had a common origin.

Prosecutor Denise Robinson had warned the jury in her opening statement that they would hear a lot about carpeting and carpet fibers during the trial, and they did. The carpet fibers found on Dawn's body were fragile and easily displaced. This meant that she had had contact with the carpeting just before or after she had died. Therefore, the carpet fibers that had been found on her body and at the dump site on East 23rd Street came from the site where she had been murdered.

"I was sick of hearing about carpet fibers," admitted Ted's wife, Linda Stuard, "but I knew it was important to the case."

Following the stipulation about John Mann's examination of the carpet fibers in 1986, the prosecution next called Dirk Shaw to the witness stand. He told the court that he worked as a trace chemist at the Marion County Crime Lab. He said that the Crime Lab now had a Fourier transform infrared spectrophotometer (FTIR). This device, he said, would tell exactly what type of fiber was being examined and would also run a spectra on the fiber. He added that, unlike in 1986, the crime lab now also had a melting point apparatus and a digital microscope. He told the jurors that he had been asked to reexamine the fibers in the Dawn Marie Stuard case, and that he took samples from every location the fibers had been collected. He then put up on an overhead projector the six samples he had tested.

Shaw told the jury, "These are the six submissions of

carpet . . . to show that they were all manufactured with specifically the same type of twist." The carpet samples being examined, he said, all had an "S" twist, which is a specific way the carpet was manufactured. He testified that all of the carpeting samples had identical coloring, even though some of them had been stained and some of them faded from age.

He then put up slides on the overhead projector that displayed the samples of carpeting laid side by side and viewed under a digital microscope to show that they were identical. Next, he put up slides of the fibers lit with special lighting to show their identical interference patterns. Shaw told the jury that he then subjected the fibers to solubility testing, measured at what temperature the fibers melted, and dissolved the fibers in acid to see what color they produced.

The results of this testing, he told the court, were that all of the fibers melted at exactly the same temperature, all of the fibers produced the same color when dissolved in acid, and when examined with the FTIR spectrometer, the spectrum showed all of the samples to be identical.

The prosecution then asked, "So after all that, what can you tell us about these fibers and pieces of carpet based on your scientific opinion?"

Shaw responded, "After all that testing I could not find anything to differentiate any of the samples from one another."

The defense had no cross-examination, and the judge excused the chemist.

Sarah Klassen, a serologist at the Marion County

Crime Lab, next took the witness stand. The prosecution used her simply to identify various pieces of evidence examined by the crime lab so that they could be entered later into evidence.

Following Klassen, Shelley Crispin testified. After being sworn in, she told the court that she was a forensic scientist in the DNA section of the Marion County Crime Lab. She talked for several minutes about what DNA was and how it could distinguish one person from another. She then spoke about restriction fragment length polymorphism, which was the type of DNA testing done in the 1990s, and how it needed a quarter-size sample in order to be tested. Crispin next told the jurors about short tandem repeat analysis, which was the type of DNA analysis used today, and how it only needed a microscopic sample in order to be tested.

The prosecution then asked her about item number 63, the blood sample taken from the brick furnace flue in the basement of the Reese home. Who did it belong to?

Crispin told the court that, minus an identical twin, the blood belonged to Dawn Marie Stuard.

Upon cross-examination, the defense asked Shelley Crispin if she could tell how long the blood had been there before collection, and she answered no. The defense then asked her if she could tell where on Dawn's body the blood had come from, and again she answered no.

Defense attorney Michelle Wall said that she wouldn't contest the finding of the DNA analysis of the blood since DNA analysis had been shown to be reliable. But, she added, she also wouldn't try to explain why the blood was there. "We do not have to come up with an alternate theory," she said in an article in the *Indianapolis Star*. "We just have to show that the prosecution did not prove its case beyond a reasonable doubt."

Following Shelley Crispin, the prosecution once again called Detective Roy West to the witness stand. They wanted to discredit the defense attorney's strategy of saying that there had been a lot of people in the house on Bosart Street that day and that any one of them could have killed Dawn.

The prosecutor asked West if he could account for the whereabouts of Paul Reese Jr. during the time the coroner said Dawn had been murdered. West answered yes, that he had witnesses who had seen Paul Jr. at the Liberty Bell Flea Market on West Washington Street during that time. The only time Paul Jr. wasn't in sight was when he left for thirty minutes, but a trip back and forth to the house on Bosart Street would have taken at least eighty minutes.

The prosecution next asked if West could corroborate younger son Brian Reese's story of being away from the house most of the day on March 16, 1986. West answered that he was able to confirm that Brian had left at around 11:00 A.M. to noon and spent the day with friends at their home at East 9th Street and North Arlington Avenue.

"John and Jeremy Reese were confined that day at the Juvenile Center, correct?" the prosecutor continued.

"Yes."

"Was Doyle Stinson ever in the house that Sunday?"

"No."

"Archie Ward and his girlfriend were in the house between 5:30 and 6:00 P.M., correct?"

"Yes."

"Besides what we've talked about, who can you place inside the house during the day of March 16, 1986?" the prosecution asked.

"Paul Reese Sr., Barbara, Jenny, Cindy, Pam, and, of course, Dawn Stuard."

"What significance did you give to Pam saying that it looked like Paul Reese Sr. had just taken a shower before she returned to the Reese house on March 16, 1986?"

"Seeing the living conditions within the home and the personal hygiene of the individuals living in the home," West answered, "I felt it was significant that Mr. Reese would have been taking a shower at that time of day."

"And to your knowledge who was the last person to see Dawn Stuard alive?"

"Doyle Stinson, between noon and 2:00 P.M."

"And that was at?"

"At 1428 North Bosart Street."

"The next person arriving at the house would have been?" the prosecution continued.

"Pam Winningham at between 4:15 and 4:30 P.M."

"And when did you first talk to Paul Reese Sr.?"

"At police headquarters at around 6:15 P.M. the night of March 17, 1986. He wasn't a suspect then. I was just trying to get some information on Dawn Stuard."

The prosecutor then went over the initial statement

West had taken from Paul Reese Sr., and after West had told the court about it, the prosecutor asked if West had taken a second statement from Paul Sr. He answered yes, and also noted that by the time of the second interview, taken on April 15, 1986, he now suspected that Paul Reese Sr. had in fact murdered Dawn Marie Stuard.

West said he asked Paul Sr. if he thought Dawn was attractive. West said that Paul Sr. answered, "Yes, she was pretty nice looking." Then West asked him if he had been sexually attracted to Dawn, more interested in seeing Paul Sr.'s body language than hearing his answer. West said Paul Sr. hesitated a bit and then replied, "No, not really, no." West found the hesitation a confirmation that Paul Sr. *had* in fact been sexually attracted to the girl.

West said he then asked Paul Sr. if there would be any reason for his fingerprints to be on Dawn Stuard. At first, West told the court, Paul Sr. said no, but then got to thinking about it and said, "Well, she had a habit of getting up on the pool table and I would pull her off."

In response to the next prosecution question, and to let the court know that the blood being spattered on the brick furnace flue had likely occurred that day, Detective West told the jurors that he had talked to Dawn's family, friends, and people associated with the Reese house. "I never learned of any injuries to Dawn Stuard around the Reese house."

The defense then began its cross-examination of Detective West. Michelle Wall asked if Paul Reese Sr. had voluntarily supplied his shoes to match against a footprint found at the crime scene on East 23rd Street. West responded that he had taken Paul Sr.'s shoes when he served the search warrant. Wall then asked, "Were all of the statements Mr. Reese gave you consistent?"

"Yes, he continued to deny involvement in Dawn's death," West answered.

"Have you over the years received tips about other suspects in this case?"

"Yes."

"Isn't it true that Dawn had some bruises before she went to the Reese house on March 16, 1986?"

"Yes, a few."

Wall then asked Detective West about how many unsolved cases he'd had as a homicide detective. West responded that he had investigated over 125 murders and had 15 still unsolved. She then asked about Barbara Reese, who at five feet four and 173 pounds would have been bigger and stronger than Dawn. Couldn't she have easily overpowered Dawn? Following this, Wall then moved on to asking about all of the people who had been in and out of the Reese house on March 16, 1986, and whether some of the timing of the events that day could be off. West said that there were no clocks in the house, so it was possible. Finally, the defense asked West if it was really that unusual for Paul Reese Sr. to have taken a shower at 4:00 P.M. West said that based on the condition of the house and the people in it, yes.

There were no redirect questions.

There was one more witness the State wished they could call: James Larry Reese, Paul Sr.'s older brother, who'd told police officers that his brother had confessed to him about having raped and murdered Dawn Marie Stuard. According to the probable cause affidavit in the case against Paul Reese Sr., James told police in 1986 that his brother had confessed to him that he'd "killed Dawn Stuard, had sex with Dawn, and he needed to get it off his chest." However, in 2012, James himself sat in an Arizona prison, serving a twenty-year sentence for child molesting. The prosecution knew that if they put James on the stand, the defense attorney, because of James's record, would vigorously attack his credibility. And so, reluctantly, the prosecution decided not to call James to testify. Therefore, following the cross-examination of Detective West, prosecutor Denise Robinson told the court that the State rested its case.

After the jury had left the courtroom, Judge Altice then had the defense and prosecution approach the bench. The judge asked defense attorney Michelle Wall if Paul Reese Sr. had made a decision regarding whether or not he would testify. The defense attorney said that Paul Reese Sr. would not be testifying.

Defense attorneys, like prosecutors, put a lot of work into murder cases and want a favorable outcome. A defense attorney must weigh what kind of damage could be done by putting his or her client on the stand, and whether the State had proven their case beyond a reasonable doubt. In this case, there had been no eyewitnesses to the crime, and a lot of people in and out of the house on North Bosart Street that day. Defense attorney Michelle Wall apparently felt that more harm than good could come from putting Paul Reese Sr. on the stand, so she rested her case without calling any witnesses or presenting any evidence.

She did this because proving a case beyond a reasonable doubt rests solely on the prosecution. It's the defense attorneys' job to show reasonable uncertainty of their client's guilt. This is often accomplished by trying to give a different spin on the evidence, by trying to raise doubt in the jurors' minds about the credibility of prosecution witnesses, or by suggesting alternative scenarios for what might have happened. All defense attorneys need to do is plant the seed of doubt in the jurors' minds and have them question the credibility of the State's case.

If even one juror won't vote for a guilty verdict in a murder trial, then the case ends in a hung jury, meaning that the jury couldn't reach a unanimous decision. The State must then decide if it wants to face the time and expense of pursuing a new trial against the accused or simply drop the charges.

Following Wall's statement that the defense rested, the judge then instructed the prosecution to begin its closing argument. In this case, the State decided that it would divide its closing argument, giving one part before the defense's closing argument, and then the second part following the defense's closing argument. The judge allotted each side sixty minutes.

Deputy prosecutor Mark Hollingsworth gave the first part of the prosecution's closing argument. He took the jury back through the case, pointing out all of the evidence its witnesses had presented. He ended his portion of the closing argument by saying, "I ask you to do justice after all of these years. Twenty-five to twenty-six years later is justice delayed. Please do not let it be justice denied. Please convict him of murder. Thank you."

Defense attorney Michelle Wall then stood up and began her closing argument. She agreed with most of the evidence presented by the State, and said what a tragedy it was, the way Dawn Marie Stuard had died. "But by whom?" she asked. "By whom is the main question in this case. I think that there are other people who could have done it. Most mainly, Junior or Barbara Reese."

Wall then went over the testimony of the trial and said that almost anyone could have overpowered Dawn. After all, she was only five feet two and 119 pounds. She also touched on DeAngelo Gaines's testimony. "I submit to you," she told the jury, "that you cannot believe anything he says. There is nothing about DeAngelo Gaines that I believe you can find credible and I think you should give it the weight it deserves, which is none."

During her closing argument, Wall conceded to the jury that Paul Reese Sr. had helped Barbara and Paul Jr. carry Dawn out in the carpet and dump her, but insisted that this does not prove he was the one who killed her. "But that is what the State has proven," she told the jury, "is that after the fact, Barbara, Paul, and Junior carried out Dawn's body and most likely dumped her in the road. But it does not say that Paul Sr. is the one who held an object similar to a stick or pool cue to her throat."

Following this, the defense discussed the timeline of that day and how Barbara or Paul Jr. would have had opportunities to kill Dawn. "Don't put that on Paul Sr.,"

Wall said in closing, "saying that he was the one who did this murder when it could have been someone else. Thank you."

Deputy prosecutor Denise Robinson then stood up to give the second part of the State's closing argument. She talked for several minutes about the case and all of the evidence and testimony. She stressed that all of the evidence the State had presented—the blood, the carpet samples, the witnesses—all pointed to one man as the killer: Paul Reese Sr. She also told the jury, "Indiana law says that flight is evidence of consciousness of guilt. The minute the Stuards came to the house, when the heat was on, he's out the back door."

She went on to say, "The truth of the matter is . . . that Dawn stayed too long and she paid for it with her life . . . We ask you to make a clear statement that this man is guilty of murder." Denise Robinson also told the jury to "hold Dawn's killer accountable. He is guilty and you know it." Robinson then quoted Aristotle to the jury: "The sum of the coincidences equals certainty."

Following closing arguments, the judge gave the jury its instructions about various points of the law that applied to the case they were deciding on. During the prosecution phase of the trial, the State had asked that "accomplice liability" be included in the jurors' instructions. This, according to Indiana law, states:

A person who knowingly aids another person to commit an offense commits that offense even if the other person:

1. Has not been prosecuted for the offense.
2. Has not been convicted for the offense.
3. Has been acquitted of the offense.

The prosecution wanted this included in the jury instructions in order to counter the defense attorney's claim that others in the house could have committed the murder. The defense attorney made no objection to this. Once Judge Altice had given the jurors their instructions, the twelve people retired to the jury room to deliberate.

It didn't take them long. After only ninety minutes, the jury came back with a finding of guilty.

Paul Reese Sr. remained stoic during the reading of the verdict; observers couldn't tell if he was surprised or not by the jury's quick decision.

Dawn Marie Stuard's father, Ted, was thrilled. "I had lived with the depression of Dawn's death for so long that after the verdict I felt lighter. I felt like a huge weight had been lifted off of my heart when I heard the verdict. Like a cloud had just suddenly disappeared over my head and the sun hit me. Finally there was vindication."

"I talked to the jury afterward," he added, "and I said you guys made an awful quick decision, less than two hours. They said that it didn't take long because on the first vote it was unanimous."

Prosecutor Denise Robinson commented that it was one of the fastest verdicts she'd seen in a murder trial during her twenty years as a prosecutor.

"Perry Mason has nothing on Denise Robinson," Ted said about her performance during the trial. "Also kudos to Roy West and Mark Albert."

Robinson gave the credit for the victory to Detective Roy West. "The Paul Reese Sr. verdict was particularly gratifying for me given the dedication that Detective West gave to the case," Robinson said. "It was his first homicide and he never let it go. In the end, he prevailed." When asked what she thought won the case, she said, "I don't know that any one piece of evidence wins a cold case—however, the DNA results certainly helped. But still, the real credit has to go to Detective West, who kept bringing this case to my attention. Without his dedication, the case would have been shelved years ago and no one held accountable for Dawn's death. I may have been the conduit to present the case to the jury, but it was Detective West's case."

Marion County prosecutor Terry Curry concurred. In a press release, he said, "The murder of Dawn Stuard twenty-six years ago is no longer a 'cold case.' While the State's charge of murder against Paul Reese Sr. was brought last year based on new DNA evidence, it was the dogged and persistent police work of former Indianapolis Police Department Sergeant Roy West which has led to today's conviction. Sergeant West, who is now an investigator with the Marion County Prosecutor's Office, was assigned to this homicide in 1986 and refused to ever give it up, ultimately bringing it to a close. We hope that today's guilty verdict delivered by the jury brings peace to Dawn Stuard's family."

As for Detective Sergeant Roy West's feelings once the case had been closed, he told the *Indianapolis Star* on June 22, 2012, "I have carried this case around with me since March 17, 1986. It has never been about Reese. It has always been about Dawn and her family. All I could think about was that child."

On July 18, 2012, the court held the sentencing hearing for Paul Reese Sr., a time when the victim's family was allowed to speak. Ted Stuard went first. He told the court, addressing Paul Sr., "On March 16, 1986, you raped, you beat, you murdered a thirteen-year-old blond-haired, blue-eyed little girl, Dawn Marie Stuard, my daughter. For twenty-six years, four months, and two days, justice has been a long time coming and today it's here . . . You started a nightmare that still persists to this day . . . Finally I can stop pursuing justice for my daughter; it's been a long journey that's going to end today . . . At the end of your life, I think justice will be well served," Ted said, looking directly at Paul Sr. "That Satan himself will come to clutch your soul and drag you off to that special place in hell that's reserved for baby killers like yourself."

Dawn's mother, Sandy Stuard (now Sandy Harrington), was too overcome with emotion to testify. Her husband, Marlin Kirk Harrington, read a statement Sandy had written. In it she said, "How do you measure this, losing your only daughter? Sleepless nights, nightmares, watching my nieces grow, marry, have children . . .

[Paul Reese Sr.], his wife, and son should not breathe another breath in this world. That would only start to be justice."

Paul Reese Sr. declined to say anything on the advice of his attorney. At this hearing, deputy prosecutor Denise Robinson also reviewed Paul Reese Sr.'s criminal record and the crime he had just been convicted of to show why he deserved the maximum sentence. The defense attorney, Michelle Wall, talked about Paul Sr.'s failing health and his remorse.

Following all of the testimony, Judge Altice said, "The court believes that the appropriate sentence in this case, for what the court in the last twelve years has seen as one of the worst, is sixty years in the Department of Corrections. The case will run consecutive to the twenty-year sentence he [already] received." The audience in the courtroom erupted in applause when they realized that the judge had given Paul Sr. the maximum sentence possible. When added to the twenty-year sentence he was already serving, this new sentence meant that Paul Reese Sr. would most likely die in prison.

Following the sentencing, Paul Reese Sr. asked the court to appoint a pauper attorney for him so that he could appeal the guilty verdict. The court approved his request, and attorney Patricia Caress McMath eventually filed his appeal. Paul Sr. based his appeal on two issues that his attorney felt were critical to his case. The first point was whether the court erred when it instructed the jury on accomplice liability, where the evidence during the trial did not support such an instruction. She said that the only evidence at the trial to support the involvement of more than one person was the effort to conceal the crime, and aid after the fact does not support a conviction for murder. The crime had already been committed.

The second point of Paul Sr.'s appeal was whether the court erred in sentencing him. He claimed in his appeal that the court imposed an enhanced sentence based on aggravating factors not found by the jury.

The court of appeals, however, on the first point of the appeal about the jury instruction, stated that Paul Sr. had waived his right to appellate review on this issue because his attorney did not object to this instruction at the trial. Even that aside, the court said, "There was some evidence that more than one person may have been involved in the crime . . . There is sufficient evidence of Barbara's possible involvement in the crime to warrant an instruction on accomplice liability in this case."

As to Paul Sr.'s second point of appeal, that he had been inappropriately sentenced, the court again didn't agree with him. They said, "We conclude that [Reese's] extensive criminal history supports the trial court's imposition of an enhanced sentence. The trial court did not err in sentencing Reese."

Consequently, the appeals court turned down Paul Sr.'s appeal. "Based on the foregoing," they said, "we conclude that the trial court did not err in instructing the jury or in sentencing Reese."

This ended the legal saga of Dawn Marie Stuard's murder. After over twenty-six years, she finally saw justice. As for the Reese family, their long legacy of crime resulted in having two members who will never see the outside of prison walls—which will perhaps save other innocent lives.

AFTERWORD

Where are all of the Reeses today?

Paul Reese Sr. remains confined at the Pendleton Correctional Facility in Pendleton, Indiana. According to his Department of Corrections fact sheet, his earliest possible release date is February 1, 2047, when he will be well past one hundred years old. At last report, Barbara Reese served her six-month sentence for the Officer Jason Fishburn incident and was released. She still lives in Indianapolis. Paul Reese Jr. and John Reese are both out of prison as of this writing, as is Jeremy Reese, who was released from the New Castle Correctional Facility the last of May 2013. Their uncle, James L. Reese, remains in prison in Arizona. He is scheduled to be released in April 2017. Brian Reese is serving his sentences at Indiana's maximum security prison in Michi-

gan City, Indiana. His earliest possible release date is
July 6, 2132.

n July 2010, the American Legion named Officer Jason
Fishburn the Indiana American Legion Officer of the
Year. As another honor, organizers selected Fishburn to
serve as grand marshal for the 2010 CarmelFest, whose
theme was "Celebrating Indiana Heroes."

However, in early 2011, Jason Fishburn decided that,
because of the disabilities he had suffered, and how much
they interfered with his work environment, he needed to
retire from the Indianapolis Metropolitan Police Department. He finally accepted that he would never be able to
realize his dream of returning to being a full-time police
officer. But even that decision was fraught with difficul-
ties. After he submitted his application for a medical disability pension, Fishburn received a shocking reply—the
state pension board offered him a disability pension of
only 69 percent of an officer's salary (the maximum they
could have offered was 90 percent).

Naturally, this controversial decision raised a firestorm
of criticism. Mitch Daniels, the governor of Indiana, and
Greg Ballard, the mayor of Indianapolis, both promised
to do what they could to see that Fishburn received a full
medical pension. "Jason had the city's back when he was
chasing that murder suspect," the mayor said in a press
release. "The city is going to have his back as he's fighting for his pension." The mayor promised that he would
have attorneys from the city's legal division assist Fish-

burn in his appeal. Eventually, the state pension board increased their offer to 79.85 percent. It still wasn't a full pension, but better than their original offer.

Today, Jason Fishburn still walks with a brace and cannot use his right arm. Although certainly not in the same physical condition he was before the shooting, just being alive, to say nothing of his ability to speak, write, read, and get around on his own, flies in the face of what the doctors who saw him when he first arrived at Wishard Memorial Hospital had predicted.

"Jason had been a very active person, and he loved his job," said his wife, Tonya. "He didn't want to go in and be a detective or anything. He wanted to be out working on the street. And for him not to be able to do that any longer, it's kind of depressing for him at times. Jason seems more emotional now than he had been. He's quieter. It's more difficult for him to learn anything new, to take on a new task. It can be frustrating for him."

However, on August 6, 2013, Jason and Tonya Fishburn found a happy ending to their troubles. Tonya delivered a baby boy, their first child. That day became a new beginning for a life that almost ended. Out of tragedy came a new hope.